# DRAMA
## FOR
# TEEN
# ACTORS

# DRAMA FOR TEEN ACTORS

CHRISTINE McCLURE

1st Edition
2023

DRAMA FOR TEEN ACTORS
Copyright © 2023 by Christine McClure
ISBN 979-8-218-20196-8

———————————

All rights reserved. No part of this book may be reproduced or used in any manner without written permission of the copyright owner, except for the use of quotations in a book review.

**First paperback edition May 2023**

———————————

EDITOR | The Editorial Department (TED)
BOOK COVER DESIGN | Premade Ebook Cover Shop
BOOK FORMATTING | GR Book Covers

# CONTENTS

| | |
|---|---|
| Introduction | 7 |
| Chapter 1  Character Building from the Self | 13 |
| Chapter 2  Being at Ease on Camera | 28 |
| Chapter 3  Incorporating the Five Senses | 38 |
| Chapter 4  Motivating Emotional Responses | 53 |
| Chapter 5  Character Behavior Improvisation | 68 |
| Chapter 6  Character Backstory Improvisation | 78 |
| Chapter 7  Working on a Movie Scene | 92 |
| Chapter 8  A Scene on Camera | 108 |
| Acknowledgements | 121 |
| Endorsements | 123 |

# INTRODUCTION

Hi there. I'd like to take you on a journey with six professional teenage actors as they study drama in an eight-week course. The actors range in age from fourteen to seventeen—the perfect age for training and transitioning to adult acting.

But before we begin, I'd like to share a story with you. During pre-production on the movie *Contagion* (directed by Steven Soderbergh), I received a call from Carmen Cuba, one of the industry's top casting directors. She wanted me to coach sixteen-year-old Anna Jacoby-Heron, who'd be playing Matt Damon's daughter in the movie.

It was Anna's first role in a feature film: a demanding character in a powerful drama. She'd be playing opposite an Oscar-winning Hollywood legend. It was a dream come true but a little scary.

We had six weeks to prepare before shooting began. In the script, Anna's character Jory is exposed to a terrifying situation: fear of losing her parents in the midst of a pandemic.

Together, Anna and I explored how she could draw on her real-life experiences to make the drama meaningful for her. We went through the script scene by scene. First, Anna improvised situations and did exercise work to help her create the logic of her character's journey. Then we worked on her behavior in long shots and in the close-ups for her emotional and revelatory moments. I knew that Steven Soderbergh didn't shoot many takes, so Anna needed to be extremely well prepared.

When shooting began, I was off camera but close to Anna on the set. I wore headphones so I could hear her clearly. I was out of everyone's way, but close enough to use the discreet hand signals we'd worked out so I could offer feedback like, "You need to show a little more feeling" or "That was great."

Anna has a beautiful stillness on the screen. We see right into her thoughts and feelings. She captured the character's fear of loss in her private moments and with her father. I was thrilled with her performance, but what really mattered was whether it thrilled the director. I waited anxiously for feedback at the end of the first day's shoot. "Spectacular" was Steven Soderbergh's opinion.

Anna received excellent reviews for her performance, and her success continues with leads in major TV series and movies, including *Newly Single*, *Finding Carter*, and *The First*.

After *Contagion*'s release, Anna sent me some lovely feedback about my coaching, which I'd also like to share:

> *Christine helped me understand the process of coming into my character and how to stay focused and ready on the set. She pushed me when she knew I could do more, anticipated what doubts and difficulties I would experience, and gave me ways to deal with them. Christine taught me so much about the movie-making details and the discipline it takes to be a professional actor. Our preparation work on my character gave me the confidence I needed. I came from our sessions together exhilarated, inspired, and in love with acting.*

If you're wondering about my own experience, I've worked as a TV and movie actor since the late 1960s and acting coach since the 1990s. As an actor, I know the US and Australian scenes well, working with some of the finest actors, agents, and directors. And I've spent more than thirty years helping young actors in some of Hollywood's most prominent productions. My job is to work closely with actors (pre-teen to young adult) to develop their skills and help them deliver great, often award-winning performances.

The actors I've coached include some of the movie industry's top talent: Yara Shahidi *(Blackish),* who's received multiple nominations and awards; Hailee Steinfeld, who was nominated for both an Oscar and a BAFTA for *True Grit;* Lexi Ainsworth, nominated for a Daytime Emmy for her work on *General Hospital*; Ashley Johnson, nominated for a Young Artist Award for *What Women Want*; Josh Hartnett in *The Virgin Suicides,* before he went on to star in *Pearl Harbor* and other productions.

My students have worked with some of the finest actors in the business:

Matt Damon, Robert DeNiro, Mel Gibson, Robin Williams, Tom Cruise, Nicole Kidman, George Clooney, Jeff Bridges, and others. And with A-list directors such as Sofia Coppola, Steven Soderbergh, Stanley Kubrick, Nancy Myers, Tony Scott, Robert Zemeckis, and the Coen brothers.

One of the reasons I love teaching young actors is that I remember what it was like when I was a young actor, starting with Shakespeare in school. In the late sixties, the Australian film and television industry experienced a renaissance, and there were new opportunities for actors. I found an agent and began working professionally in 1969, using the stage name Elli Maclure.

In 1977, I was offered a US film role and traveled to Los Angeles. It was like another world and I had to work my way up, starting with supporting roles in film and TV. I had the privilege of working with some of Hollywood's best, including director Francis Ford Coppola. He told me during a meeting that I needed to have a videotape of myself playing a character with an American accent. (At that point, my reel was purely Australian.) He chose a scene for me to do, and we taped it at his Zoetrope Studios. Not long after, I won a role in a play, *Love Streams*, with the innovative and revered actor/director John Cassavetes, starring Gena Rowlands.

My career turning point came in 1989, when I began studying with John Lehne in Los Angeles. John was a well-known character actor, a member of the Actors Studio, and a renowned acting coach. He'd studied with Lee Strasberg, the great American teacher of "method" acting, and brought his own unique innovations to the training process. Inspired and supported by John, I decided I wanted to teach young actors.

I called my approach "Method for Young Actors," which caught the eye of agents and managers representing young professional actors. Agents knew that many of the great adult actors had trained in method acting, and I soon I had a busy schedule of acting students. My approach proved successful, and I earned a reputation in the business. On one occasion, Iris Burton and Chris Snyder (the premiere agents for young actors at the time) called to thank me for my work with their clients. Iris asked me, "What do you do? Get into their heads?" She was right; that was an excellent way to look at it. Method is the inner technique.

In Hollywood, young actors are thrust into an adult profession, and their skills need to hold up onscreen when they are working with actors who have decades of experience. As a teacher, I need to prepare them to meet this challenge. At some point, I learned that directing an actor on "what to do" doesn't necessarily produce the best result. The actor needs to know how to do what they're asked to do—*how* being the operative word here. My students learn to motivate a character psychologically, behaviorally, emotionally, and imaginatively. That's what this book is about: giving you the opportunity to "see" my method in action—and gain insight by following these teen actors in dramatic roles.

In the pages that follow, you'll read about how teen actors create dramatic roles through exercise work, character improvisation, and scene work. After that, the actors will reveal what they worked on, their goals, and their insights—followed by class questions, discussions about their acting experiences and, finally, my feedback and guidance. We do this in a safe environment where students feel free to make mistakes, learn without being judged, support their dreams, and share their love of acting. Those who train in this method will be educated for life because they know how to construct a role.

It is my hope that reading what these talented teens accomplish will inspire all young actors to develop the skills they need to meet the film industry's demands and achieve their own goal of becoming great dramatic actors.

~ ~ ~ ~ ~ ~ ~ ~ ~ ~ ~ ~ ~ ~ ~ ~ ~ ~ ~ ~ ~

Acting feels natural to me, and I'm exceedingly grateful to work in a profession I love. There are ups and downs, of course, too much work at some times and too little at others, but this is where

I belong. I've met some of my best friends in the industry, and many people who've been extraordinarily supportive: those early producers and directors in Australia, my teacher in the US, and the agents and managers who believe in the work I do for their clients. Some of the most joyful moments of my life have come from watching young actors perform with boundless energy, fearlessness, creativity, and wild imagination.

All my best,
Christine

NOTE: There are no " " marks on most of my own words in class because I didn't want the book to read like one long conversation.

# CHAPTER 1

## CHARACTER BUILDING FROM THE SELF

Actors:

| | |
|---|---|
| Maya | Josh |
| Asia | Deion |
| Hayley | Jacob |

MEREDITH FINE, A LEADING AGENT FOR YOUNG ACTORS IN Los Angeles, once asked me, "How do you work with the actors?" I told her, "I find a side to the actor they can use to play the character. That makes them real in the role." After that conversation, I decided to write this book based on my experience and an upcoming, eight-week dramatic acting class with six professional teen actors: Maya, Josh, Asia, Deion, Hayley, and Jacob.

As an example of how the actors should approach the classes, I thought of a teen girl experimenting with a character from the film *Hamlet* (1948), directed by and starring the great Laurence Olivier. The teen actor is massively impressed by Ophelia, played by Jean Simmons. The film is old, but then Shakespeare's *Hamlet* has inspired actors for four hundred years, and the acting and direction in the film are timeless.

My teen actors settle into class. I look at their expectant faces and greet everyone by name. Then the lesson begins.

I say: I'd like to begin with an example of a teen girl who explores different sides of herself to become a character. Then I'll give you an exercise to do. Based on your performance, I'll know what you need to work on next for your individual development. You're all at different levels, so what one actor needs will differ from another. The benefit of a class is that you learn from what you experience in the acting process. You might have ideas about what to do, but you won't know if they work until you try them and get feedback. You'll also learn by observation and by taking part in other actors' exercises. All these things will bring you insight into your own acting work and experience. As will my own feedback and guidance, which comes after. All the work we do here is based on drama. So let's begin.

I'd like you to picture a fourteen-year-old girl with long dark hair, alone in a boarding school dormitory. It's winter. Bitterly cold air blows inside through high arched windows. The girl wanders between the beds in her nightgown, her bare feet on the wooden floor. Her body shakes and her feet are almost blue, freezing in the cold. She thinks about the way Jean Simmons played Ophelia in Shakespeare's *Hamlet*. Ophelia doesn't care how she feels in that cold castle in Denmark, so the girl stops shaking and tries to separate her feelings from the chill. She spins around and sings whatever comes to mind, making up words and melodies. When she stops, the giddiness makes her feel like she's floating. She wanders the dormitory with that feeling, disconnected from the world.

She stops next to a chair. She remembers the film: how the chair reminded Ophelia of where Hamlet sits in the royal court, and how the actress reached out above the chair as if tracing Hamlet's face with her hand. The girl does the same thing, and slowly moves her hand along the side of the face she imagines in that space. She's overwhelmed with sadness. Tears come to her eyes. She didn't expect to feel that. She pulls her hand back and holds it over her heart for a few minutes.

Then she breaks character, shakes her hands to get warm and pulls a blanket around her like a cape. She smiles, loving the experience she just had—the acting.

Because she'd been inspired by Shakespeare's story and the actors' performances, it wasn't enough to just watch or think about what she'd seen. She wanted to feel like Ophelia, to be her and to feel real as her.

Not only did she experiment with what it felt like to be that character, but she also did some preparation beforehand.

She knew there were vast differences between herself and Ophelia. They were close in age but led very different lives: the girl lived in the twentieth century in a boarding school and Ophelia lived in a sixteenth-century royal castle in Denmark. So the girl needed to find ways to relate.

In her research, the girl saw that Ophelia lived near the North Pole, so she decided to experiment using a cold day in her environment. In Ophelia's final scene, she was alone and adrift in the world, mourning her father's death and suffering Hamlet's violent rejection, with no mother to lean on for support.

The girl was young and innocent. She'd never experienced romantic love like Ophelia had with Hamlet, but she had felt rejection from people she loved. She didn't consciously create rejection or think about what happened to her personally.

Instead, her pain surfaced unconsciously when she did the actions and used her imagination.

She didn't have the training to motivate her feelings when she needed them, like professional actors do. With no fundamental understanding of psychology or how to work on Ophelia's descent into madness, she found her own way by observing the actress in the film, empathizing with her, imitating her actions, and imagining a face in the space above the chair. The physical act of spinning was the only way she knew to feel out of touch with reality, so that's what she did, imagining it must feel like that to be mad. As a result, she successfully motivated different sides of herself to help her transform herself into her idea of Ophelia. She took her first steps toward becoming a character.

In class, Asia raises her hand and asks, "How did the girl come up with the ideas to do what she did: the spinning, imagining being there, trying not to feel the cold, and the idea to imitate?"

Desire to act, I answer. The girl loved what she saw and wanted to discover what it felt like to be Ophelia. Others love the film too, but not everyone will try to be that character. I believe that desire is your talent. We don't know where talent comes from exactly, but that doesn't matter. What matters is what you do with your talent. Your desire urges you toward action in your life—actions like coming here to learn. Some of you have already acted professionally, but you're here because you know you have more to give and you want to learn how to do that. Ask yourself: Is there a character you dream of playing, from a book or movie or script—or maybe even someone you saw in school or on the street? Something that inspires you and makes you imagine what it would be like to be that person? The best way to discover how to become a character is to act the character.

When you explore a character's behavior, listen to that voice inside when it tells you to do something. When you have an impulse, act on it. Give yourself the freedom to follow the impulses we normally ignore to be socially correct. Don't worry about whether your acting is right or wrong, or what anyone thinks of you. Just explore and discover. Follow your impulses, open yourself up to the possibilities within, and find new sides to yourself so you can play a wide range of characters.

Now, actors, let's get on with the work. First, I'd like you to do a short exercise. I want you to create the behavior the girl did when she explored how to be Ophelia. Use imagery in the empty space—the face of someone you love and would miss—and do the same physical actions she did, reaching out to the person you imagine sitting in the chair. Or you can spin around to experiment with what it feels like to lose touch with reality. Let's see what you discover and what side of yourself it motivates. After the exercise, tell me what you experienced, and I can guide you on what you need to do going forward.

I tell the actors that for this exercise, they'll work onstage, one at a time.

The stage is at eye level with the seated class, but I ask the actors to work in the center or close to the front. That makes it easier for the other actors to observe small details, and it helps my evaluation.

Go onto the stage area, I say. Put a chair in front of you if you choose to imagine the face ... or use the stage to do the spinning and walking.

Let's start with Maya, then Josh, Asia, Deion, Hayley, Jacob.

Jacob speaks up, "I'm kind of new to acting. Is it okay if I just watch for now?" I tell him yes, of course. And Josh asks, "Am I meant to play a girl like Ophelia?"

I see the other teen boys looking a bit confused too.

Good point, Josh, I say. You don't have to play it like a girl. This is not a character exercise where I expect you to create someone different from you. It's a motivation exercise to see how you respond to imagery and physical actions. Remember, I say to the class, when doing this exercise to surrender to whatever happens mentally, emotionally, and physically. You will all have different reactions because your personal histories are different. So let's just see what happens.

One by one, the actors go through the exercise on the stage.

Maya concentrates on touching an imaginary face in front of her. After a moment, I see she's a little frustrated with herself. She pauses, looks at the space above the chair, and reaches out again, but her frustration returns. A few minutes later she gives up, looks at me, and shrugs. I gesture for her to sit beside me, and I whisper, "Don't worry. You did well. I'll explain later."

Josh looks at the chair and puts out a hand. Then he pulls it away, shakes it, and laughs to himself. He takes a moment to look back at the chair. I watch him roll his eyes, walk away, and lean against the wall, thinking as he looks back at the chair. He's holding onto the feelings that were motivated and staying involved in the exercise.

Asia reaches into the space above the chair, then quickly pulls her hand back and steps away. While she looks at the chair, her eyeline changes from the seat to the space above the chair. She turns her head as if watching someone walk away and struggles to hold back tears.

Deion grabs the imaginary face in his hand and leans close, as though looking into someone's eyes. Angry, he squeezes the face and knocks the chair over—catching it before it hits the floor. His body looks tense as he firmly puts the chair back and stands there with a threatening look.

Hayley spins around for a while. When she stops, she steadies herself then walks around tentatively, unsure and light on her feet. Next, she stands still and gazes out over the class to the back of the room. She looks around—then stops still again. She thinks for a few moments. Then, overcome with sadness, she bows her head and covers her face with her hands.

I look at the actors, feeling fortunate to see their commitment to acting, their imagination, and their willingness to explore and experiment—and the different results that one small exercise can create. It's going to be a fantastic journey with this talented group.

Great work all of you, I say. It is extraordinary to see what you created with an image and physical actions. You were all creative, focused, and made discoveries on the stage. Maya, let's start with you and what you have to say about your experience in the exercise.

## MAYA

Maya is still concerned about her performance, but she speaks up. "I imagined seeing my little sister in the chair. I thought of the time when she was in a terrible situation. I was so upset my mom didn't know what to do with me. But when I imagined my sister just now, I didn't feel upset like I did when it happened. But then when the feelings didn't come back, I panicked and worried I wasn't doing it right. I felt bad."

I am sorry you felt bad from the exercise, I say. But consider it a good thing that you had this happen in class, where we can solve the problem. Now let's look at what you wanted to do: recall feelings you felt in the past. How long has it been since the situation happened, and has the situation changed since then?

"It was two years ago," Maya says. "Our family had a terrible time when it happened, but everything's okay now."

I give her my feedback, saying the positive thing about the exercise is that you didn't fake the feeling you wanted to recapture. Don't ever fake; always work with what you honestly feel. It's a mistake to listen when someone tells you to think of when your dog died and try to recapture that feeling. You can't recreate exactly the same feeling because as you grow older and have different experiences, how you relate to the past changes too. In the class on motivating emotional responses, you'll learn that feeling is always a present reaction to a past experience. You'll also learn how to arouse emotion when you need it. If the exercise you did just now were a scene in an upcoming movie, and you need to be emotional, you'll be able to do that with the work I mentioned and repeat it whenever you need to.

I turn to the class. Actors, I say, we'll work on exercises for emotion in great detail. But it's not something that can be learned quickly, so it's going to take some practice.

I look back at Maya and say: For now, what you did helped me see what you need to work on next. What I want to work on with you is how you feel in front of an audience. What we do here will also apply to acting on camera.

"Good, because I get nervous," Maya says.

I look at the class. Remember, I say, in class, try not to expect too much of yourself in the exercises, because this can lead to feeling frustrated and block your creativity. We don't want any negative feelings getting in the way of your dream to become great actors. Making mistakes and not knowing what to do can be a good thing because you can learn from that. The industry expects you to know what to do, and you're judged by what you do—which is why I don't allow anyone from the business side in my classes. I don't want mistakes held against you. In this class, you'll have the opportunity to learn more about yourself by opening yourself up to the possibilities within, stretching your talent, and learning from guidance. You'll start growing as an actor, until you're ready to take on any role that comes your way.

I ask Josh to go next.

## JOSH

"Well … I felt a bit stupid doing the exercise," Josh admits. "I tried to imagine someone I love and would miss. My brother came to mind. We fight but still love each other. When I was doing the exercise, I didn't want to touch his face. I probably wouldn't do that anyway in real life. So I just decided to go with feeling ridiculous. I knew not to stop. Directors mostly want that too. One time a director yelled at me, 'Why did you stop? I loved it!' Which was weird because I thought I was terrible … that's it I guess."

I tell him he did the right thing using what he felt and continuing the exercise. Staying with it, I say, allowed me to see how you work. And talking about what goes on with you when you're acting. You told a story to anyone looking at you. We saw a boy frustrated by what he was looking at and leaving the situation. We draw conclusions based on what you do. We can't hear what you're thinking; instead, we see you act.

"So when I play a character," Josh asks, "I can think anything, as long as it makes me behave the way that person would?"

Exactly, I say. You can think whatever you like as long as it motivates the character's behavior. It's best to use this kind of work as preparation. For example, I've suggested to an actor to use counting backward for a character who needs to be deep in thought. And once in a character's frame of mind, use that feeling as the bridge to a scene. Then think like the character. The imaginary circumstances will enrich what you already feel from your preparation.

Josh, what I want to work on with you is how to find a side of yourself that can behave like the character, even if you haven't had the same experience as the character. Then you can try the exercise again with this new technique. We'll work on that in the sensory class.

"I'm ready," he says.

I look at Asia and ask to hear from her.

## ASIA

Asia thinks back and feels the space again before speaking. "When I put my hand out to touch him, I felt my feelings change. Then when the person I was looking at, the person I was remembering, walked away, a thought came that I didn't plan. I tried to stop the feelings because I didn't cry when the situation really happened. But the tears came anyway."

I tell her that her emotion was beautiful and very real. I ask if she'd be okay telling the class more about the situation.

"Yes," she says. "I was thinking about my dad; he's in the military and has to go away a lot for his job. I'm aware of what could happen to him if he went to war but try not to think about it because it is too hard, so I remain optimistic."

I speculate that she denies or suppresses her feelings when the real situation happens—but felt those suppressed emotions surface in the exercise.

Asia nods. "Yes."

I see her feelings surfacing again and ask if she's okay to continue. She takes a deep breath and says, "It's okay. We worked on roles before where I had to cry a lot. They want that when you're a child actor. But now I'm older, and I need some more situations. Some of the early ones don't affect me much anymore."

I tell her she's a brave girl and say: Would you be willing to explore the situation with your dad again in an emotional exercise in another class and add the thought that came up for you just now?

"I think so," she says.

It's important that she feel confident. I tell her that feelings are delicate, and I want her to feel safe. "I want to do it," she tells me. I let her know she can do the emotional exercise two classes from now. I ask again if she's ready, just to make sure. She nods.

I tell the class that what I'll be asking Asia to do is a skill they can use their whole lives. Now you're teen actors, I say. Your roles will be more challenging than the ones you did as child actors. And the roles you'll get in the future will be more challenging than the ones you're doing now. So we're not just working to make you better teen actors; we're also training you for your adult careers. Some of these exercises will be painful, but we'll work on a technique to turn your feelings on and off at will so you don't hold on to difficult situations.

I turn to Deion and ask to hear from him.

## DEION

"What was great about this exercise was that I finally got to do what I wanted to do to that person," Deion says. "Squeezing the face kept my muscles tense, and it helped my anger. The other thing was I didn't want to break the chair, letting it fall on the floor. So I kept my body tense when I grabbed it, so it looked like I was still angry. I hope it worked."

I tell him it did, that the way he used the image to arouse his feelings and how he reacted physically were excellent. I believed everything he did. I asked him if he knocked people off chairs in real life.

He smiles. "No, but a couple of times I wished I could have. The impulse was there. But I know I can't behave like that."

I tell the class that acting isn't what we do in life, but what we want to do. Think about it. We have many thoughts we can't act on, but in class we can. Uncovering impulses helps you get to know yourself. You see how those impulses lead you to behave, then later, you use that behavior to create a character. I tell Deion that what he did with the chair was very professional.

"The stunt guys helped me when staging fights," he says. "I have to look like I'm hurting the actor without really hurting them."

I tell the class that, like Deion, they need to respect the guidance of fight trainers and choreographers and other experts. Then I tell Deion he's ready to take on a challenging role and ask him to think of a character he's never played before. It can be from a movie or television drama. Begin by improvising the character's life before they appear in the script. In other words act the backstory. For the first improv, try walking, sitting, and thinking like the character. Next set up how the character behaves in their daily life. After that, explore the character's relationships. The aim is to develop the character before doing a scene.

Deion nods. "Got it." After that, I look to Hayley and ask her to tell me her experience.

## HAYLEY.

"When I did the spinning," she says, "I did too much on purpose, so I had to work hard to center myself and walk. I'm glad I did it. Like the girl in the dormitory, I don't know much about mental illness, and I haven't had losses like Ophelia. But after doing that I felt ... not mad, but different. Like I was ... delicate, that's the word. Like I could break easily."

I nod my head and tell her: Yes, I saw you change physically and emotionally. You drifted, like you were in a world of your own. There was a beautiful moment at the end where you were overcome with sadness. You covered your face with your hands like you wanted to block out your feelings. What happened there?

"I did feel sad," she says. "The story you told affected me—what it must be like to lose everyone you love and not have a mother to turn to. Although I wasn't even thinking about that in the exercise. But when I was standing there, the thought hit me: 'What will I do?' I felt helpless. There was nowhere to turn. I wanted to hide."

As Hayley speaks, I see her emotion surfacing again. I say it's beautiful to see her so affected. What we all hope for in acting, I continue, are those spontaneous moments that make your work come to life. You allowed the story and the physical actions affect you, and surrendered to your impulses. Your ability to do that helped you gain insight into the character. That's good work.

I ask Hayley if she's read *Hamlet*. She shakes her head and asks if I think she should do a scene. I tell her she read my mind and say I'd like her to work on Ophelia's last scene in the play for our character class at the end of the course, which will give her plenty of time to study. Still, she's cautious. "Do Shakespeare?" she asks.

Absolutely, I say. You've already found sides to yourself that allowed you to play Ophelia. Look how much understanding you brought to her through a simple exercise. First read the play straight through to get an overall idea of the story. Always do that with movie scripts too. You don't have to make sense of every word. Give yourself plenty of time. It is a long play. Also, watch the movie with Olivier, which will help you understand the story better.

And after that, I say, study Ophelia's scenes. If you don't understand specific phrases, look at what's said before and after. For the scene I mentioned, Ophelia's last scene, you can continue to work on the behavior you started here in class. You already have ideas about her physicality and glimpses into her emotional life. Now work on how she ends up losing her mind. If you like, the scene can be on camera.

An on-camera scene will help you see how your behavior on the screen can tell the viewer more about Ophelia than just what's in the dialogue.

"This will be a challenge!" Hayley says. I agree, then tell her I have great faith in her abilities.

### JACOB

I then turn to Jacob, who was nervous about his first class and just watched the others. I say, I don't want to push you into anything you're not ready for, but I'll think of an exercise for you for next class, if you feel up to it. He seems a little reserved, but tells me, "I'm in."

~ ~ ~ ~ ~ ~ ~ ~ ~ ~ ~ ~ ~ ~ ~ ~

I see Asia and Maya whisper something to each other. Then Maya looks at me and says, "Were you the girl you talked about in the beginning?" I was, I tell her. I've acted for many years, and I started when I was very young. Otherwise, how could I help you?

# CHAPTER 2

BEING AT EASE ON CAMERA

Actors:

Maya—being-at-ease exercise     Jacob—improv with Maya

Asia     Deion

Hayley     Josh

MAYA OCCUPIES A CHAIR ONSTAGE, FACING THE CLASS. I tell her to relax and be herself; there's no need to act a character or situation yet. Just be aware of what's going on in the class around you, I say, and surrender to any impulses that may come. I will tell you when to stop. Ready?

## MAYA

Maya focuses on a spot in front of her. After a few moments, she sits up and looks left then right. Then she slumps back in her chair. Her right leg shakes: she's nervous. She stops it with a hand, breathes out and relaxes. Then laughs. "I have no clue what I am doing," she says. She gazes at the floor, then to me. "I feel like I should be doing something." I tell her to keep going, and she relaxes again and stares into space. I thump the floor with my foot, but she's lost in thought. I thump the floor again, louder this time. No response. I tell her she can stop now.

"This was hard," she says.

Yes, I saw that, but you persisted. To help you understand why I had you do this exercise, I want to backtrack a bit before we talk about what you just did.

Remember when you did the Ophelia exercise and imagined touching a face to see what that motivated? You were disappointed, so you gave up and looked at me. Why do you think you did that?

Maya thinks it over. "Well, I felt like I wasn't doing it good enough. I guess looking at you was asking for help. I did the same thing in this exercise. With everyone watching, I guess I wanted to, you know—look good."

I thank her for being so honest. Admitting that, I say, will help you know what to work on when you have those thoughts again. And believe me, we all have fears about acting and how we look to others. Right? I look around me.

"For sure I do," Hayley says, and the others agree.

I look back at Maya. There are several things to look at, I say, when it comes to what you did in the first class: touching an imaginary face. You hoped that feelings you had in the past would return, and when the feelings didn't return, you looked at me and wanted to give up. Right now I want to work on the feeling of wanting to give up, which happens because you allow your awareness of an audience influence your feelings about yourself. I want you to feel good about yourself and feel free to do your work in front of an audience and on camera, without worrying about what anyone thinks of you.

Now let's look at the current exercise where you were sitting in the chair. You had some tension in your leg, which you were conscious of, and tried to stop it.

"That happens when I worry about something." Maya says.

It's good you were aware of the tension, I say, and you could relax in the moment. You sit in the chair as you, as Maya, to help you feel free to be yourself in front of others. Just be you—and take in anything that happens. Understand?

It clicks for her. "So, I'm not supposed to act anything imaginary but just sit and be present—feel, hear, or see whatever's going on. When I heard the thumping noise, I needed to react to it. Instead I tried to ignore it because the noise wasn't part of any acting scenario. It was part of my experience in the chair. Right?

Yes, I tell her. Maya asks, "Can I try again?"

Of course you can, I say. But before you do that …

I turn to Josh and Asia and ask them to bring the table that is at the back of the classroom onto the stage. They pick up the table and bring it to the stage. "Where do you want it?" Asia asks. I think for a moment and say: Please take it to the back of the stage. They do that. I tell them to stay where they are. Moments pass.

Asia looks at me suspiciously, wondering what I'm up to. Josh gets it. "I see what you're doing," he says. "We thought you meant get the table for real. So it wasn't like we were actors doing an exercise, which might have changed how we behaved. Instead it felt natural, that is until we became conscious of everybody looking at us."

Right, I say. You did what was asked of you, in front of the class, and never gave it a second thought. Then when you stopped and looked at everyone looking at you, everything changed and felt awkward. When you're aware of being watched, it changes the way you feel even if you're not looking at the people who are watching you. Have you noticed in real life that some people don't like being photographed? What is it about putting a camera in front of someone that changes how they feel? For some people, it feels like an invasion of privacy. Others love the attention and start posing for the camera. Either way, there's a change. Why is that? I look to the class for answers.

Deion speaks up, "Something to do with conditioning?" he asks. "I can be in a crowded room, walk into a shop, or come home and not be bothered by someone looking at me to say hello. I'm used to that. But it's rare for someone to look at me closely, unless they see I'm emotional or behaving in a way that attracts attention. I guess we go about our lives without feeling eyes that are on us all the time. But when we're acting, it's like people look at us closer."

Great answer, I say. The difference between how you behave in life and as an actor is that you know you're not just being casually observed but scrutinized. Every detail, thought, feeling, and action is closely observed—onscreen, on set, onstage, in an audition, and even in a class like this one. You can't escape it. The audience watches because they want to be captivated by what you're doing, and they want you to reveal more to them than they see in real life. It is your job to give them that. Which is why you have to be unafraid. That's the only way you can be fully expressive and bare your soul with everyone watching.

I scan the room, my gaze settling on Hayley. When you started acting, I say, did anything change when you became aware of being watched?

Hayley smiles, knowing we worked on this problem together. "Sure, I was eleven, and came to you to tape a role for an audition. When you were coaching one-on-one with me, it felt great. Then when you set me up in front of the camera to tape the scenes, it was hard to feel as emotional as before. I kept forgetting the lines, which made me tense. Finally you asked me to do twenty jumping jacks to loosen up and punch the air to reconnect to the angry feeling I had to do. After that I relaxed and didn't worry about the camera. And I got a callback from the tape."

I remember, I say, and tell her she's flourished ever since.

Hayley smiles again "When I came out of the coaching, my mom asked, 'How was she, how did you do, did you like her?' And I remember saying it was weird, I did physical things and my acting was better."

I say there are many exercises an actor can do to help them perform. That's true of seasoned actors as well as beginners because there's always an adjustment when facing an audience or a camera. I ask Maya to repeat the exercise.

She sits back in the chair and breathes out. Her leg shakes briefly, but she acknowledges it, relaxes, and looks me in the eye. I see a bit of challenge there. She takes in the room but doesn't push things. Her behavior seems natural. While Maya looks elsewhere, I signal Deion to walk onto the stage. He does. Maya turns and watches casually as he strides past her chair. He walks out of her sight, goes to the back of the stage, and waits. Moments pass. Maya starts to feel awkward with Deion behind her. Eventually, she turns to look at him. She smiles and turns away, waiting to see what happens. A few minutes later she gives up and turns to Deion again. She shifts to one side of her chair and beckons him to come sit beside her. He does. They look at each other, amused. I tell them they can stop there.

"That was fun," Maya says. "I felt like I could go on forever and still come up with things to do."

It was fun to watch you too, I say. The performance was relaxed, you started from where you were and you were present for whatever happened. You interacted in the situation as it unfolded and followed your impulses. Don't be afraid to be vulnerable and surrender to whatever you experience in the moment. It's easy to love you when you're open and honest with what you're experiencing. Allow us to love you for who you are. It may be uncomfortable being yourself in front of others when there's nothing to do because that's not what you thought acting was. But we do this exercise so you can work through the uncomfortable until it becomes comfortable. You'll be working in front of others your whole career, and it's part of your training to feel good about that. As an actor, there must be the desire inside you to be looked at, noticed, and loved, right?

Maya nods, a little shy to admit it. "Everyone wants love. But I guess I have to feel okay even if people don't love what I do."

That's absolutely right, I say. Working this way paves the way for later, when you'll be creating your characters. You cannot separate yourself from the character you play because you and the character become one. So acknowledge what arises inside you. We can't plan every moment of our lives, so we learn to adjust to the unexpected moments. When we're acting, there will always be spontaneous impulses. You need to feel entitled to express those. That's what makes the acting unpredictable. It's for the audience to watch you and wonder what happens next.

Which, I say, brings up another point I want to discuss. Do you, as an actor, feel entitled to be in front of an audience? Do you feel like you have a right to be there? Have you heard the expression, "own the room?" An actor often hears this when heading to an audition. It means you're being encouraged to take the time you need to bring out the best of yourself to create your vision of the role. Think about how you feel when preparing for a role at home. You feel free to be yourself and do whatever you feel like when exploring your character. You need to get to that same feeling when you're in front of an audience or on camera. My teacher used to say, "We do our best acting in our living rooms." So let's make your on-camera work as good as it is at home, or better. Thank you, Maya. You did excellent work.

## JACOB

I turn to Jacob. Are you ready to work? I ask.

"Definitely," he says. Great, I say. You will act in a simple situation—as yourself, not as a character. Maya will do this exercise with you.

Jacob, you come into the room, see Maya, and say the opening line: "Hey, how are you?" Then improvise by coming up with what to do in the moment. When you hear me say "repeat" I want you to go backstage, then come back in and say the line, "Hey, how are you," in a different way and improvise again.

"So after the opening line, I just say and do whatever until you tell me to stop?" he asks.

Correct, I tell him.

Jacob goes backstage, and Maya remains in her chair. A few moments pass, then Jacob walks in and stands beside her with his hands in his pockets, taking a moment to look at her.

She glances at him, then looks away so he can't see her face. He waits another moment, then says, "Hey, how are you?" His expression is soft, like he senses there might be something wrong. When he gets no response, he sways on his feet wondering what to do. "Awkward," he says quietly.

I tell him to repeat.

Jacob walks out. After several moments he comes back in and strides across the stage and plants himself right in front of her. "Hey, how are you?" He is super friendly. Maya shrugs her shoulders and turns away again. Jacob changes tactics and says, loud and angry, "Hey!" She looks back at him, playing off his anger. Defiant, as if they just ended a fight. Jacob challenges her, saying firmly, "So, how are you?" Maya says, "Fine," and they glare at each other.

Okay, I say. Good work. Let's hear from the two of you. Maya?

"I don't know why I decided not to say anything. It was a bit rude, I know, but I just went with it. I felt freer acting, though."

It shows, I say. You surrendered to impulses, relaxed in front of the class, and interacted with another actor with ease. You've made progress. Good work.

"Thank you," she says. I look to Jacob and ask how he felt.

"Well, I was pretty scared before I walked in," he says, "this being my first time doing anything in class. But planting my feet on the floor and putting my hands in my pockets helped me feel like you said, 'own the room.' Trying to see what Maya was thinking helped me lose the awareness of you all looking at me because I concentrated on looking at her. I was aware of you and the class several times but didn't try to fight it.

"In the second improv, when I came back in, I was determined to get a response. When Maya didn't answer, I felt the impulse to get mad, and the words just happened with that feeling. I lost my awareness of being watched when I felt angry. I guess the emotion takes over. It's like going in and out—I am aware one moment and not the next—but I wanted to hang in."

Great work, I say, adding that he gave us a great summary of his work. I welcome him to the class and say, what a great start. I'm impressed with how you went through the exercise and surrendered to what you felt in the moment. And with how you waited until what you felt compelled you to speak, so the words came naturally. I want you to remember what you did and use that same method to approach your scripts. Now, why don't you tell us when you first wanted to act?

Jacob says, "A year ago. Our English teacher at school is a big Shakespeare fan. He had us all do a speech from a play. I decided on *Macbeth,* and to do the scene when he is having visions about wanting to kill the present king so he can be king. In the 'is this the dagger I see before me' speech, on performance night, as I said, '… thus with his stealthy pace/With Tarquin's ravishing strides, towards his design/Moves like a ghost,' I looked out over the audience and pointed, slowly moving my hand to follow this evil ghost walking there. I could feel the audience quiet, waiting, watching. Suddenly I grabbed for the ghost. Someone gasped. It felt great to hear that. After that I loved acting."

I ask if being aware of the audience helped him. He says it did; it made him put more feeling into his role. I ask whether the others have had moments like that. All of them have. I tell them that involving your audience is part of the actor's job. Actors are here to share what the great Russian director and teacher Konstantin Stanislavski called "the extraordinary moments in the life of an ordinary man." You can't let the awareness of being watched block you from sharing all you have to give—with your insight and how you want your character to be seen by those who watch.

Think of your audience and what you want them to experience, then bring that into your work. You might be thinking: Can I just lose myself in my character and not have to worry about all this? Yes, there will be times like that when you go through deep emotions, perform with other actors, and focus on physical actions—and that's ideal. But there are also moments when you think of all these things. No matter how lost in a character you get, you still need the discipline to be aware of the technical aspects, too—like the blocking, the lights, your other actors, directions—all while being aware that others are watching. Share yourself with the audience. Give all you have to give in your roles.

That's it for this class. Excellent work and input from all of you.

# CHAPTER 3

## INCORPORATING THE FIVE SENSES

Actors:

| | |
|---|---|
| Hayley—improv using the senses | Josh—personal-object exercise |
| Asia | Deion |
| Maya | Jacob |

The actors are scattered around the stage. I tell them they'll all be working at the same time and to find a spot where they have some space.

In this class, I say, you'll be working on how the five senses—sight, hearing, smell, taste, and touch—motivate an experience. You can choose which one of the five senses you'd like to work on. There's a table with some objects to use: bags of ice cubes for touch, bottles of vinegar for smell or taste. You can also use the rough walls for touch. For hearing, listen to the sounds inside the classroom and outside the building. For sight, I will give you an observation exercise with another actor.

While you're working, I'll walk around to see what you're doing and guide you if necessary. Ready? Let's begin.

I get Josh's attention. I say I'd like him to work on touch and have an exercise for him to do later. Something to help overcome the awkward feelings he had in the first class when touching an imaginary face.

Josh moves to the side of the stage. I walk closer to observe him. He moves his hand across a small section of the rough plaster wall—back and forth, back and forth—then it stills. Josh looks at me. "What should I do now?" he asks. I tell him to imagine he is touching the wall. He moves his hand in the air the same way he moved it on the wall. I ask if he feels anything, but he shakes his head. I guide him through a repeat, telling him to explore the physical sensations slowly. Break down the feeling into small parts, I say. Feel where the rough bits affect you and make a mental note of it. As he moves his hand he says, "It's tingling where the rough is." Good, now take your hand away and try to recreate the same sensations, I say. Josh moves his hand over the imaginary wall. "I feel the roughness of the plaster. Not exactly the same feeling, but something." Better, I say. Keep working. I look to the rest of the class.

Deion stands with his eyes closed, listening to sounds. I walk toward him, and he turns to listen to my footsteps. He senses my closeness and asks, "Is that you, Miss?" Yes, I say, and ask him what sounds he hears inside the classroom and what sounds he hears outside the building and on the street. Deion thinks. "Outside—the cars, a child crying, hammering. In here—your voice and Josh's, a buzzing sound I think is from the lights. Maya kept saying 'yuck,' and I heard you walking toward me."

Now do the exercise with your eyes open, I say. I tell him to recreate one of the sounds in another part of the room—like moving the car sounds to the ceiling or the floor. He focuses on the effort.

I walk over to Maya and Jacob standing next to the table set up with the bottles of vinegar and ice cubes in plastic bags.

Maya smells vinegar, and her face and whole body twitch. I ask her to recreate the smell without the vinegar. She smells the imaginary vinegar and twitches again, just as naturally as the first time.

Jacob pours a bit of the vinegar on his tongue. His reaction is mild. "I don't mind it," he says, "and the taste is still in my mouth, making it easy to recreate." I ask him to name a taste he doesn't like. "Liver!" he says. His face and mouth move like he has trouble swallowing. "My friend's mom cooks it," he says, "and I have to eat it to be polite."

When you said "liver," what came to mind? I ask. "I saw some pieces on a plate and my mouth reacted," he says. I ask him to recreate the liver here on the table, then try tasting it. Jacob concentrates on a spot on the table, then picks up the imaginary liver, puts it in his mouth, and chews. "It's repulsive," he says. I smile.

Then I go to where Asia holds ice cubes tight in her hands. She does that for several moments, then drops the ice and places her cold hand on her forehead. "This feeling of the cold reminds me of something," she says. Good, I say, let us know about that in the feedback. I then walk to where Hayley is also working with ice.

Hayley has a bag of ice cubes beside her on the floor. She slides a handful of melting ice over her leg. She looks like she's in pain. "It hurts," she says. I tell her to take note of the difference in temperature: where the cold affects the body compared to where the body feels warmer. "Can't feel it," she says. So I tell her to try a different part of her body. She holds the ice on her neck. "I definitely feel the difference now because my neck is warmer," she says. Good, I say, and think of how you can use the "hurt" feeling for an acting situation.

I look around the stage and see that the actors have worked through their sensory exercises. I tell them to pair up and face each other. I say: You'll be working on seeing. Take a partner and stand opposite each other; then, I want you to observe the other person. Concentrate on their face.

They partner up on the stage: Jacob and Deion, Asia and Maya, Josh and Hayley. I walk around and observe, asking questions: Have you noted the expression in your partner's eyes, their eye color, whether their hair is long or short? Are they wearing jewelry? What clothes can you see close to their face? What's the shape of their face?

After a few minutes of this, I tell them to turn away from their partners and trace the shape of their partner's face in in a clear area in front of them. Keep the image close to you, I say, so that nothing can distract you. I observe Jacob struggling to recreate Deion's face. Look again, I tell him, and this time look at his hairline and where his ear meets his cheek. Next, I ask the actors to look at each other again. This time, I say, I want you to look into each other's eyes. See what the other person is thinking or feeling. See if you learn more about them by making eye contact.

I watch as the actors face their partners and do the exercise. When it's over, I have everyone sit on the stage and tell them I'd like to hear what they've discovered. We start with Josh and his exploration of touch.

## JOSH

"Breaking down the effect of the plaster wall on my hand into smaller parts gave me something to concentrate on," he says. "There are so many details in touching something that I never thought about. I became more aware. When recreating the touch on an imaginary wall the strongest sensation was the easiest to feel. I learned that I need to imagine something specific."

Yes, exploring your sense of touch did focus you. Your work improved when we asked questions about what you touched. Questioning what you do makes you more observant; it helps you focus on the details and examine them.

I continue. Now let's look at what we began in the first class, I say. After you did the Ophelia exercise, when she imagined seeing Hamlet in the chair and reached out to touch his face, you said doing that made you feel a bit stupid. Right?

"Yes. I guess I'm not a touchy-feely person," Josh says.

I say: Your acting will improve if you stop thinking that way about yourself. Let's see if the sensory exercises will help you. Sensory work gives you different ways to arouse emotions and remove emotional blocks. It helps you to know yourself. Once you do that, you can use the emotional responses you discovered in new roles. The goal is for you have control over your body so you can play anything. Acting is not about what *you* would do under the circumstances, but which side of you to use to *become* what you need to play that role in those circumstances. Let's try something. Is there anywhere in your life where you feel comfortable using the sense of touch? Take your time.

After a moment he says, "My dog, Casey, I pet her a lot."

I ask how old Casey is, hoping we're on to something that might help.

"She was a stray, but the vet thinks she's around fourteen, almost as old as me, I'm fifteen. I've had Casey practically my whole life."

I answer: Do you have any thoughts about her getting old and what it might mean?

Josh thinks it over. I give him a moment. "Like she might die soon? It's hard to think about that," he says. Then I set up his next exercise, saying: I want you to imagine Casey is here next to you and you're petting her. Feel your hand stroking her fur and let thoughts come to you. Other senses will come into play, too, like seeing her hair color, the look in her eyes, any sounds she makes.

Josh sits down on the floor and reaches out like he's stroking Casey's head. He pets her slowly, concentrating on his hand, then takes a moment to look at her—and moves closer, as if looking into her eyes. His expression changes. We see his lips tighten as he holds back emotion. He takes a deep breath and looks away, then breathes out. "Wow, I didn't expect that," he says. "My throat closed up when it hit me she might be dead in a few years."

I tell him he did good work. Strong feelings were aroused in you, I say, beginning with your sense of touch. From there, you followed your instincts as if Casey were here with you. But before any other comments, I'd like to work on getting the emotion past your throat. So stand up, shake your body, stamp your feet hard, and yell until you're exhausted. Put all your energy into it.

"Really?" he asks.

I nod. Josh shakes all over and stamps and yells until he's tired and I tell him to stop. I tell him to scrunch up his face, then relax it—and to repeat that several times. When he does, I ask about the tension in his muscles.

He shakes his arms, legs, and shoulders, turns his head from side to side to stretch, then releases the muscles in his neck. He breathes out. "Better," he says.

Good, I say. Now I want you to sit back down and imagine you're petting Casey again. Then add the thought of losing her forever. When you feel the emotion in your throat, breathe out and add the sound "*Ahaaah.*"

Josh pats Casey by imagining she's there. He leans close, looking into her eyes. I see his feelings changing. "Ahaaah," he says.

Louder, I say.

"Ahaaah!" he says again.

One more and even louder, I tell him. Surrender to your thoughts as you stroke Casey.

"*Ahaaah.*" His voice chokes. Then he says "*Ahaaah*" again and again. Finally, all his feeling comes into his voice and breaks into a sob, and his face changes as he's overcome with emotion. He looks up, in tears. He wipes them away, still a little afraid to show his feelings.

You see what's happening? Your feelings surfaced when you released the tension in your body. Tension is built up over time to hold back our feelings. Starting when we're told "Don't cry" or "Don't yell." So we tense our muscles to stop the tears or raise our voice. Relaxing the muscles allows the full expression of emotion to pass through them. Add the breath release, which carries the voice, and the effect grows stronger. You also moved through the psychological barrier of letting your vulnerable feelings show. You expressed your emotion in your voice, face, and eyes. This kind of expression is where the audience sees your characters' most difficult moments in your thoughts, feelings, and decisions—in close-up on the screen. As actors, you need to focus your feelings there.

A few more points, I say. What also helped with using the sense of touch is that you know and love Casey. She's part of your daily life. You often see and pet her, which makes it easier to imagine her. Casey is what we call a *personal object*. We all have personal objects in our lives. It could be a photo of someone you love, a gift you'll never part with, a pet, a song, a place, or something like the chair that reminded Ophelia of Hamlet. Personal objects are valuable to the work because of their power to arouse emotion.

I address the whole class, saying: When you work with personal objects, know that we can't predict feelings. We might hope that imagining something or using an object will arouse what we want to feel, but then we try it and get a different response. In all your sensory work, allow whatever you feel to come through, and surrender to it. Don't try to steer it in the direction you want it to go. Instead, work with the personal object until you've explored how much feeling you have in response to it. Then repeat it. If you get an emotional response each time, then that is a reliable preparation you can use when playing a character.

I call Josh for one last exercise, telling him to reach above the chair, like he did in the first class—and to add the feeling he discovered with Casey.

Josh reaches out, concentrates, and gently touches the space in front of him. His expression is soft, his movements relaxed.

Then he lowers his hand, looking sad, and stares at the spot he touched. Then he smiles. "So much easier this time," he says. "I didn't think of Casey. It was more like I knew the feeling to call on. Does that make sense?"

It does, I tell him. Then I ask how else he might use this feeling.

"If I have a script that asks me to gently touch my deathly ill mom's face in a hospital bed, I could use this same feeling. The actress is a stranger, but it wouldn't feel like that because I'd feel the love I feel for Casey."

Exactly, I say. Superb work, Josh. Thank you. Now let's hear from you, Deion, about your work on hearing.

### DEION

Deion reflects on his work. "It seemed like my concentration was better. I picked up more on the differences in sounds: the highs and lows. I wanted to turn toward the sound to know what it was. Moving the sound around was hard, but I get why we do it. Now when I see a sound mentioned in a script, I can listen to it in real life then come back to the script. They never give you the sounds on set, so that's a way to make it feel more real …

"Sometimes, when I'm acting? It's hard to get totally into it. But I see how to get better. When I hear another actor speaking, I can ask inside my head: Am I listening? Just now, listening, I felt like I was totally into it. That's what I need to do in the roles."

I add: When you are listening to the other actors, thoughts arise that motivate your feelings and affect how you interact with the other characters.

I tell him he makes good points. You gained insight into using sounds in your scripts, I say. And you discovered the difference between hearing and listening. Hearing you do naturally; you don't have to think about it. But listening, that's where you focus on the sounds and what they mean. You listened to my walk, turned toward it, then went on with the exercise. But in scripts, every sound is there to tell a story, and how you react tells a part of that story for the audience.

Deion nods. "So when I hear a gunshot, figure out where it came from, and duck for cover, that's part of a story."

Exactly, I say, impressed with how deeply these teen actors immerse themselves in the exercises. I tell them that using their senses helps them work moment by moment. Sounds are heard and listened to; thoughts follow, then actions. Any questions?

Deion shakes his head. "That about covers it," he says. I turn to Maya and ask her to share what she discovered by working on smell.

## MAYA

"The smell affected me," she says. "I hate vinegar. I usually avoid things I don't like. The exercise made me realize I've never really thought about how my senses work. It was pretty amazing when you asked me to imagine smelling vinegar and I reacted like it was real."

I smile, remembering her twitch response. Yes, I say, you had a strong response and were able to recreate that without actually smelling the vinegar. And that's what we aim for in sensory work. How could you use this same feeling for a character?

"The way the vinegar made me act?" Maya asks, then thinks again. "Something that makes me twitch? I could be like this girl at school who overreacts—moves around and pulls faces—when she talks about someone she hates. I could imagine the vinegar smell to motivate that. No one would know I was thinking about vinegar. They'd just see me pulling faces like I didn't like something. Or someone."

A perfect example, I say, and ask if she remembers when I told Josh in the first class that an actor can think anything, as long as it puts them in the character's frame of mind. She does.

You use the sensory stimuli as a preparation, I continue. Thinking about vinegar during the scene would distract you from what you need to do: interacting with the other characters, imagining the environment, remembering the direction for moves. You need to trust that when you-the-character talk about the person you hate, your preparation will rise to the surface.

"So I need to be good at the behavior from the sensory stimuli so I don't have to think about it when I'm in the role."

Right, I say; you need to practice. I address the whole class: Practicing conditions your body to behave the way you want it to when you're in front of the camera. Use something real at first, then imagine it. Spend a part of every day just getting good at recreating what you see, hear, smell, taste, or touch. No matter where you are: the more places, the better. Pay attention to how you respond in real life, then think about how you might put those responses to use in other ways—like Maya with her vinegar.

Be careful not to leave your sensory work until the last minute, when you need to motivate your character's behavior. Great actors write and talk about working on their characters' behavior for months before the cameras roll. In television, you can go from audition to casting really fast, so you need to make the most of the time you have when it comes to figuring out what you need for that role. Which is why I recommend having a list: it gives you a menu of proven choices, things you already know will work for you. And the more experienced you become, the bigger that list gets.

I tell Maya she's done good work, then turn to Jacob and ask him to tell us what he learned from working with sight.

## JACOB

"When Deion and I were looking at each other," he says, "and you asked the questions, that helped me pay attention and see more things. But when I traced Deion's face in the space, I had to look at him again to get it right."

I tell him he's made an important discovery. Looking at someone, I say, can be meaningful, but generally, a look is when you turn around or glance. *Seeing* is when you spend more time to study someone.

Jacob, what happened when you looked into Deion's eyes, and what did you see in his expression?

"He was nice," Jacob says. "I felt like he was welcoming. We held the look for a bit, then Deion grinned, then I grinned, and it turned funny and we laughed. Even though he's a way more experienced actor, I kind of got from him that we're in this together."

I nod. Eyes do tell a story, I say. You were affected by what you saw and learned something more about Deion. Actors use this silent communication in their work. As screen actors, when you have very little rehearsal time, often the other actor in your scenes is not on the set until it's time to do blocking for the camera. There isn't a lot of time to get to know their interpretation of their roles. So when you are acting the scenes, seeing into another actor's eyes helps you to quickly tap into what they're thinking and feeling. Making eye contact is one of the best ways to communicate.

Seeing and hearing are the most used of the five senses we have—but don't underestimate the others.

I tell Jacob that his thoughtful approach to the exercises indicates that he'll go far. I ask Asia to tell us about her experience with the ice.

## ASIA

"When I was working with the ice," Asia says, "something happened. When I put the ice down and experimented without the ice in my hand, and I touched my forehead with my cold fingers, it reminded me of when I was young and how my mom would stroke my forehead as I fell asleep. Her fingers always felt cold on my forehead. So I tried to imagine that, and I could feel her hand again. I felt a calm feeling spread all over me. I haven't thought about that for ages."

Isn't it interesting, I say, that we don't know what will happen or how we will respond until we try something? The ice motivated you in a way you didn't expect. Still, the good thing is that you knew to surrender to what your body was telling you, which allowed your thoughts and feelings to come through. And out of that came a beautiful memory of your mom. But how could you use the "calm" feeling in another way other than the situation with your mom?

Asia thinks, then says, "I could be a calm character who is like that as her personality, or someone who has to calm down if she's upset."

I tell her good work. And everyone be aware that you can't predict the outcome of a sensory exercise, just like you can't tell yourself what you want to feel. You need to explore and be open to whatever comes. You'll discover sides of yourself that you can use to create new experiences.

I thank Hayley for being patient and ask about her experience with the ice.

## HAYLEY

"The cold feeling from the ice penetrated right into my body," she says. "First through my hand, but then it sent a spiky feeling all over me, like torture. I thought I'd get used to it, but I didn't. After I put the ice down, I had to rub the cold off me. I had this awful feeling, like when I wear wool. I can't stand that; it's spiky like the ice."

I decide to dive in with a behavioral exercise. I ask Hayley to recreate the effect of the ice and use that in an improvisation.

Hayley goes onto the stage. After a moment, she rubs her forearms and legs, frantic, trying to make the spiky sensation go away. Her feelings build. She looks up, as if seeing someone terrifying looming over her. She backs away, pushing something, until her back is against the wall. She looks around, filled with fear and seeking escape. Suddenly she screams: "Get away from me! Get away!" She calms down over the next moments.

I ask her to tell us about what she just did.

Hayley sits down and breathes out. "I just let myself run with it. I wanted to rub that horrible spiky feeling off me. I imagined an evil prickly creature with iron spikes for hands, grabbing my arms. It kept coming at me and wanting to eat me, like I was in a horror movie. This sensory work is powerful. At first I thought it was weird. Now I see the reason for it. We don't know how much is in us until we experiment."

I tell her she did an excellent job, that she was imaginative and I believed her fear, then I address the whole class.

Look what you all did working with the five senses, I say. You discovered something new about yourself and how to change. That will help you play a wide range of characters.

And practice—because there's no point in doing a sensory exercise once. Any skill takes work. Can you imagine being able to play the violin without practice? So for another exercise, look around yourself when you leave here. See the clouds, hear the birds and smell the flowers, touch the leaves, taste the water. Then recreate it all so you can live in an imaginary world just as easily as in the real one.

Be observant of people too. Actors need to develop insight into human nature by studying others. Try to work out what motivates their behavior. Doing this, you'll also gain a better understanding of the characters in your scripts.

# CHAPTER 4

## MOTIVATING EMOTIONAL RESPONSES

Actors:

Asia—emotional exercises + cold read

Josh—cold read with Asia

Maya

Deion

Hayley

Jacob

I BRING UP THE FIRST CLASS, SAYING: ASIA DID AN EXERCISE where she imagined someone she loves sitting in the chair, as Ophelia did with Hamlet. Asia had a thought about her father that made her very emotional. At the time, I suggested she should explore that reaction further. She'll do that now, with an exercise involving affective memory. Briefly, the purpose of an affective memory is to discover the actor's present reaction to a past experience or an imaginary experience.

Asia has been doing this exercise for three years since she started working with me at twelve. She's used affective memory successfully in her roles. I think seeing the technique in action will be helpful.

Many young acting roles call for a lot of emotion, I tell them, especially "crying on cue." In movies and TV, the scenes are short and you don't have time to build into the feelings, so you need to have the emotion ready and waiting before you act the scene. This exercise for motivating emotional responses will help you do that.

When I first studied with John Lehne, a renowned method-acting teacher in Los Angeles, I saw affective memory in action and wondered what was happening onstage. It seemed strange to see an actor sitting on a chair, wholly immersed in some invisible experience they were witnessing in front of them and saying, "I see that, I hear the sound, I feel my heart pound." When I saw the actor become completely overwhelmed by powerful emotions, I thought: Wow, I wish I'd had this exercise when I was younger. Adapted for teen actors and using the same technique with imaginary experiences, affective memory has become a big part of my work.

One more note before we begin. Because these exercises are more advanced—arousing emotional responses, and in the following classes for character development and scenes—one of our more experienced actors will play a lead role in each class and work with the rest of you. Everyone has a part to play.

I ask Asia to sit on a chair onstage. Remember, I say to her, you are not trying to recapture the same feelings you had in the first class exercise. Explore the situation with your dad again as if it is occurring now. I might talk to you during the exercise, and you can ask me what to do if you need help. Ready?

## ASIA

Asia sits on a chair, hands resting on her lap. She breathes out, relaxing and getting comfortable. She keeps her eyes open, focusing on a space in front of her and not catching anyone's eyeline.

Asia takes a moment to recreate a situation, then says in a matter-of-fact tone of voice, "I feel my arms, my feet, I see his face, his eyes, the expression, his smile. I hear his voice. I feel his hand, my shoulder, the weight there." She pauses for a moment. We can see that something's affecting her, but she keeps going. "I hear what he's saying. I feel my chest." Her breathing changes, and she holds her breath.

I tell her to breathe and relax.

She breathes out, keeping her focus on the experience. "I see his jacket, the color. I see ..." She seems to have lost the feeling she had before. She shakes her head, about to give up.

I tell her to keep going and say: Go back to the moment when your dad's hand is on your shoulder. Start there and dig deeper with more sensory details. And try not to stay with one sense.

She continues. "I feel his hand, my shoulder, the weight, hear his voice. I feel my chest, tight, I see him turn, see his back and head. I hear his footsteps. I feel my heart. I see his hand, the door. I have a thought, I feel ... pain, my heart, I see the door move, hear footsteps." Tears come to her eyes, "I have a thought." She presses her lips together holding back her feelings.

Relax your lips, I say quietly. She does. Stay focused on what you are looking at and that thought.

"I see his hand, the door. Can I say the thought?"

Yes, I tell her.

"What if he doesn't come back?" she says, and the tears come to her eyes again. She has connected to a deep emotion.

Seeing her close to a breaking point, I ask her what she wants.

"I don't want him to go," she says.

What do you want to happen?"

"For him to stay, I want my dad to stay."

Tell him, I say.

"Stay!" she calls out, crying. "Daddy, I want you to stay!" Calling out her feelings overpowers her. "Stay!" she calls out again and completely breaks down, but she stays focused on the image.

I tell her she can stop now. Now, I say, take your mind off the experience. Try not to hang on.

She lets go of as much as she can and focuses on the classroom, which is still silent with the impact of her emotion. I ask if she can tell us what happened.

"My dad is in the military," Asia tells us, "and when he says goodbye, he puts his hand on my shoulder. That's what I felt. I'm the oldest, and he always says, 'Take care of your mama and brothers.' I say, 'I will' and try not to show any feelings because I'm trying to be responsible. He's home now, but I decided to picture him about to be deployed to a war and imagine what it would be like if it that was the last time I saw him. I have that fear but I try not to think about it. We don't talk about that at home because we believe it's an honor to serve. I admire my dad and hang onto the thought he's doing good for our country … but my fear is always there of what could happen to him."

I tell her that the work was brave, then turn to the class, saying: It's important to understand that this emotional work with an imaginary idea is delicate and personal. I want to make sure you know how to use it safely. That means knowing how to turn the emotion on and off at will so you don't go too far and wind up in pain after the exercise. You'll feel pain when doing the exercises or playing a role because that's your job: feeling what the character experiences. But you must be able to turn it off when you're done, by concentrating on something else. Also remember that just because you imagine something doesn't mean it will happen. Clear?

The actors nod. Jacob raises his hand. "I thought what Asia did was incredible, but it scared me. Do we have to do this exercise?"

No, I say. You don't have to do anything that makes you afraid. Not until you're ready to break through the fear. The greatest obstacle to your development as an actor is trying to do things you're not ready for. Right now you love acting. Let's keep it that way.

I turn back to Asia. Your work is excellent, I tell her. We will talk about it in more detail when we open a discussion in class.

I address the class: Let's look at why you use imagination. Your imagination—thoughts about what *could* happen—can be controlled and called upon at any time. When doing this exercise for emotion you need to find situations that won't change, so you can rely on that situation to motivate your feelings every time you need it for a character you are playing.

To find a situation that won't change, look for relationships where you have a long history, like someone you've known all your life. By the time you reach your teens, your feelings for that person are a big part of you. You'll have ups and downs, but your overall feeling for that person is constant. Just like Asia and her dad: she's clear on her love for him and imagined what could happen. You saw how deeply that affected her. Imagination is a powerful tool. Until you are adults, I'd prefer you use imaginary ideas; it's more reliable, and some past situations are best left alone.

Hayley speaks up. "So use someone I know and just imagine something?" she asks. "I can't use an experience from the past, even though I'm sixteen?"

You can use a past experience, I tell her. But you need to test your present reaction to that experience to discover the outcome. Emotion always comes from what you feel now. As you grow and change, your feelings do too, so how you relate to people and situations changes as you get older.

If you recreate the past hoping you will feel the same emotions you felt then, it doesn't work that way. You may still have strong feelings about a past situation that had a big impact in your life, and it will always affect you, but as time goes on … those feelings could fade or even get more intense, but they are changed.

What you are learning to do with any work on emotion is for you to feel what your character feels. Actors on screen can't fake feelings or simulate it by pulling a face or acting it in their voice. The audience sees every detail of your expression. And you can't fool them; they've seen too many great actors being real.

Josh asks, "Can we know what we want to feel before we do this exercise?"

You won't know the outcome of an affective memory until you try it, I say. You can't steer emotion in any particular direction or force yourself to feel something. We can't tell ourselves we'll cry at four o'clock. You need to think of something to motivate yourself. Maybe you can cry if you've a bad day. But when you play a character, you have to deliver the required emotion, good day or bad. This is why you need to have an emotional preparation you know will work for you so when a director calls action, you have your feelings ready. So plan ahead. Build a repertoire of affective memories you can draw on when you get an audition or acting job.

I ask if anyone has questions.

Josh says, "Why did you ask Asia what she wanted?"

I answer, looking at the class: I asked Asia what she wanted when she was at a breaking point in her emotion. We saw her tears, but did we really know what was causing that? It was when she called out to her dad to "stay" that we understood what was motivating her to cry. What you want is not always clear. To discover that, ask yourself what you want when you are at the breaking point emotionally. You might have to verbalize a few ideas until you have fully revealed what you want to say. Then say it. And keep the "I want" in the positive rather than saying "I don't want," which can hold you back from expressing your innermost feelings.

Jacob raises his hand. "So doing this exercise, it's not like I'm watching myself and another person in a movie. I have to feel like I'm in it?"

Yes, I say. Feel yourself present. Think back to when you explored the sense of taste and thought of the liver, and it repelled you. It was like the liver was in your mouth, right? That is what you do with this exercise.

"Okay, I get it, thanks."

I hope his interest will help him get through his fear of the exercise.

Maya asks, "Why do we speak out loud in this exercise?"

So you can connect your feelings into the sound of your voice, I say. We will understand how you feel by your tone. And you will feel completely expressive.

Josh says, "I usually close my eyes when preparing feelings, so that's not good either?"

Right, I answer. Keep your eyes open to connect the imagery to the space around you. Don't just think of a situation in your head; you need to experience the circumstances and the people in your affective memories like you're right there with them.

Maya asks another question: "Why do we sit still instead of acting out the situation?"

I answer: So you can use your emotion in other situations. Sitting in the chair helps you to relax and concentrate, and you free yourself from the actions you did in the situation you are recreating. Muscular movement can distract from that. When your emotion flows easily, you can then add it to movement and an activity.

Then I think about how to demonstrate that, saying: You saw how Asia recreated a situation with her dad and how emotional she became. She didn't act out the situation. She used her senses to explore it while she sat in the chair. Let's see how Asia uses those feelings in another circumstance.

I pass a book to Asia and ask if she's ready for more work. She is. I tell her to remain in her chair and repeat her affective memory.

When you feel ready, I say, start looking at the book's pages. If you feel an urge to move, just surrender to whatever comes to you.

Asia focuses on the situation with her dad and the imaginary thought. We see her emotions build. She opens the book and turns the pages but is too upset to read. Her head tilts down. Tears fall on the pages. Then she snaps the book shut, gets up and puts the book on the chair. She walks to the front of the stage and looks out over the class like she is looking at someone in the distance. The powerful emotion of loss she had before overtakes her again.

After several moments I tell her she can stop.

Asia sits down facing the class. I ask her to tell us how she aroused her emotion and how it affected her movements. She thinks back.

"I started where my dad had his hand on my shoulder," she says. "Then I opened the book. As I was turning the pages I imagined he was leaving and I saw his hand on the door, and the thought came of never seeing him again, that's what upset me. When he was gone from the room I couldn't sit there any longer, so I went to an imaginary window and saw my dad walking away outside my house. I didn't imagine the window when I first did the memory, but still seeing my dad helped me feel more, and I kept thinking, 'I want you to come back.'"

Thank you, Asia. I say to the class: Asia did her sensory work silently. But when you first practice arousing emotion and adding in movement, it helps to speak the sensory language aloud, like I see, I hear… while doing a task like picking up books or folding clothes, then practice thinking of the sensory details while silently still doing those same tasks. This prepares you for when you need to add emotion to a character's actions in a situation.

Now let's look at how you can use an imaginary affective memory as a preparation for a scene. Asia and Josh, I'd like you to do a cold read of a scene from a movie script.

I search through several scenes I have beside me on a chair while Josh joins Asia on the stage. I give them each the scene to read. Your characters are Lily and Dylan, I say.

While Asia and Josh study, I say to the newer actors, Jacob and Maya, that a "cold read" is when actors act scenes from the script with very little time to prepare and without being able to read the entire script. Doing a cold read is when you really need to follow your instincts and have emotional preparations ready.

I turn back to Asia and Josh. Ready? I ask.

## ASIA AND JOSH

Asia stands opposite Josh. She takes a minute to prepare her emotion almost to the breaking point. She'll use this moment as a bridge to acting the scene. She faces Josh, and they begin the scene.

EXT. SUBURBAN NEIGHBORHOOD—NIGHT

The houses are dark and set back from the road, with big front gardens and giant trees. The street is deserted.

LILY (Asia), angry, swings around and walks away quickly from DYLAN (Josh).

DYLAN. (Calls out). What was that about?

LILY. Dylan, quiet! Everyone will hear you.

Lily stops and looks anxiously at her grandmother's house. The lights are on. Dylan walks closer to her.

DYLAN. I'm trying to be your friend. I wish you would talk to me, tell me what's going on with you.

LILY. I have to go.

Lily turns to walk away again. Dylan grabs her arm to hold her back.

DYLAN. Come on. Let's not fight.

LILY. I'm not fighting.

She throws off his hand and tries to go around him, holding onto her feelings. Dylan moves to block her from walking away.

DYLAN. Then what is it? Have I done something?

LILY. No. It's not you. Please, let me get past you. Can you get out of my way? Move!

DYLAN. All right, I'll move and pretty damn fast.

He strides to his car.

Lily watches him, then, with a sudden change of feeling, runs after him. She grabs his hands, desperate to hold him back.

LILY. Don't go, please. I didn't mean it. It was a shock seeing my mom. I won't be like that anymore, I promise.

Her changing emotions frighten Dylan, but he tries to be calm, kind.

DYLAN. Let's just call it a night. A lot has happened. Seeing your mom after so many years must have been difficult. I'm sorry if I made it worse, but … you'd best go in.

LILY. Stay with me. Please, please.

DYLAN. We shouldn't. It wouldn't be right. Let go, Lily. It's late. Your grandma expects you home by now.

Lily breaks down crying.

LILY. Please don't leave me, Dylan. Please. Stay with me all night. Somewhere.

DYLAN. We can't. Come on. I'll walk you to the door.

Lily lets go of his hands, head down, humbled, vulnerable. She shakes her head: No, don't. She wipes her tears and walks away on her own.

Dylan watches her leave, concerned.

Asia and Josh take a moment to let their feelings subside. When they're ready, I ask them to take a seat, and I ask what they discovered during the cold read.

Josh goes first. "Wow! Working opposite Asia, with all her feelings, gave me so much. When she said, 'Don't go,' it was like when she called out to her dad, but obviously this was a teen fight. Her emotion hit me so hard I wasn't sure what to do, even though I haven't read the whole script, but how I responded to Asia felt right. It was kind of like dealing with my little sister when she gets emotional."

I saw your struggle, I say, which is right for this character. You have great instincts, Josh, and you follow them. You said Asia gave you a lot, and I could see how it helped you interact. But what do you do when you have an audition with a casting director who reads the lines without emotion because they want to see what you can do?

Josh thinks it over. "I'd prepare the feelings ahead of time by finding a way to identify with Dylan. Then reading with the casting director, I'd look in their eyes and relate like they're going through the same thing as the Lily character."

Exactly, I say. As well as auditions, when rehearsing alone at home, or when you work on a movie in your close-ups, you may need to generate the character's emotion without the other actor there to help you. Fantastic job, Josh.

Asia, can you tell us what you experienced in the scene?"

Asia says, "When I prepped and reached the feeling of wanting my dad back, I went into the scene. I didn't think of my dad in the scene, but of what was going on between Dylan and me.

"Lily seemed upset right from the start, which made me think that something bad happened to her before, so a strong feeling would work. I struggled to hold back at first, like Lily did. But when Dylan walked away, it hit me that I needed him. I wanted to stop him, and the strong feelings just spilled out. It's like the scene added to what I was already feeling. I really wanted him to stay."

Asia, I say, now can you think back to your affective memory and tell us what moment motivated you to want your dad to stay? And whether you used that moment to prepare for this scene?

Asia is perfectly clear on this. "Seeing my dad's hand on the door and having the thought that I might not see him again. I used that moment to prepare."

I thank her for being so open about what went into it. Then I talk to the class: The hand on the door is called the *key object*, which can be anything: a look, sound, touch, taste, smell, thought. And when she concentrated on that key object before the scene, she aroused her feelings in one minute.

Next, the moment Asia felt the emotion rise in her to "I want," that was her feeling from the affective memory—and her bridge into the scene. When you feel compelled to say or do something, that's when you act. The action you perform is how we understand what your character experiences in that moment.

A final point: what Asia did by *not* thinking of the affective memory during the scene was correct. Instead, she involved herself in the imaginary circumstances and trusted that her preparation would work for her. And it did. Of course, sometimes the emotion might come from a different place than what the screenwriter describes, but that's okay if the outward impression—what the audience sees—is the same.

Does anyone have any questions?

Deion asks, "What's the clue to finding the right affective memory when a character has a very emotional scene in a script?

Look at how your character is feeling and what that makes them want, I say. Then your "I want" in an affective memory needs to parallel what the character wants. The "I want" might not be written, so you need to work it out. In the scene you just saw, what do you think the girl wants?

Deion reflects for a moment. "Well it seems like the girl has been without a mom for a long time. Even though she pushed the boy away, when he wanted to leave she ran after him, like she was afraid of losing him. If someone has those issues I'd say she feels unloved. So yeah, she'd want love."

Right, I say. And when working on motivating emotional responses, think in terms of opposites. If you want love, then imagine a situation where it is taken from you.

Deion nods, "Got it."

As working actors, you play deeply emotional characters. The question to ask yourself is: Am I willing to explore fearlessly, and touch on things that might be painful to deliver what the script demands? From your class participation, I'm confident you are.

Affective memory work for motivating emotional responses is invaluable. The best feedback I receive about actors' work always comes down to the fact that they learned how to motivate an experience. That creates a depth and believability in their characters that they just couldn't reach before.

# CHAPTER 5

## CHARACTER BEHAVIOR IMPROVISATION

Actors:

| | |
|---|---|
| Hayley | Deion—behavior exercises |
| Asia | Josh |
| Maya | Jacob |

### DEION

DEION WALKS QUIETLY ONTO THE STAGE. HE STANDS THERE, allowing his feelings to pass through him. He walks around, stepping lightly. Then he sits on a chair and leans forward, resting his arms on his knees.

Deion's eyes widen and he gazes around the room. He looks young and innocent. The feeling in his eyes gives us the impression he's at the teenage stage where the world is opening up for him. He stays like that for a few minutes, thinking.

When the exercise ends, I ask what character he's working on.

He answers, "I wanted to act out my first impression of the character from a mini-series script I read a couple of years ago. In the first scene, there was a moment when I felt myself change—a feeling that made me want to move a certain way.

When I was preparing the character for class, I felt the same feeling come back in my body as when I first read the script. Now I'm discovering if I break out of that physical form, I don't feel like him. It's like I need to move … quietly. Lightly.

Then a new feeling happened just now. When I sat forward, I felt excited, like I was looking forward to every day. I connected to his thoughts. I'll use that feeling as a starting point to explore the character when he's fourteen."

I nod. Could you tell us about your character?

"He's Kevin Richardson, one of the five exonerated teens in the *When They See Us* series. It's based on a true story. The performances are incredible. It's kind of intimidating to do the character after watching a great young actor in the role. But I want to find out if I can do this character, so I'm doing it anyway.

"The boys were proven innocent in 2002. Since then, filmmakers and journalists helped get their story out, so it was easy to find the details. Ken and Sarah Burns made a documentary about it called *The Central Park Five*. Then Ava DuVernay did the limited series. Even the police video of Kevin's final statement is on YouTube.

"But at some point I had to stop and just explore the character by acting."

Deion ducks his head, holding onto the feelings that hit him talking about what happened.

We wait. I allow Deion time. When I feel he's ready, I ask him what he's feeling.

"Helpless, angry, pain," he says. "The more I think about it, the stronger that gets. The fact that they managed to deal with being imprisoned for crimes they didn't commit and survive is ... inspiring."

I agree. The real story is horrific, I say. So it's good to work on stories like this in a safe environment. Sometimes you'll be working on scripts and characters that will be hard to face. These drama sessions will help you prepare for whatever challenges lie ahead. The more the feelings fill you up, the more effective you can be at using them in your acting. But remember to practice turning your feelings on and off; you don't want that stuff in your head full-time.

When Deion had first considered working on this character, I say to the class, he called me up and asked if I thought it was okay to play a real, living person. I wrote to Ken and Sarah Burns at Florentine Films. They provided an email introduction to Kevin Richardson, who was very gracious and gave us the go-ahead.

Note: [Plus, I informed Kevin Richardson that I would be writing about the actor's character work in my book on drama.]

I look to Deion. Did you know about the five boys and what happened to them before the series? I ask.

Deion shakes his head. "The whole thing happened in 1989, before I was born. I found out about it when they were casting the series. I read the script but didn't audition because I was working on another show. But the story stuck in my mind, so I wanted to work on one of the characters in class. I decided on Kevin."

I nod. You've made an excellent start, I say. When you were onstage, I saw a boy who was younger than you and moved differently, cautious and quiet, but with hope. Is that how you see the character?

Deion smiles. "Yes. Whenever I see the adult Kevin in interviews, he is kind of quiet, so I feel on track with that side of him. But I'd like to see what happens in my next exercise. Should I set up now?"

I give him a thumbs-up.

Deion goes to the stage area and moves objects and furniture into place. As he does this I talk to the class.

What Deion just did I call a *first impression* exercise, I say. After you first read a script, put it down and sit quietly. Give yourself time to think back over the scenes. As you do this, ask yourself: Did any feelings come up or did you connect to what the character was saying, or does an image of a person come to mind or remind you of someone? Or was there a moment like Deion had when he felt how his character moves? Those first thoughts and feelings are instinctive and give you a starting point for creating your character.

When you trust your instincts and act on them, it builds faith in your own creativity. You have many clues in the scripts, but in the long run it is you, the actor, who gives life to a role. And what better way to start than by searching within you?

I ask if the class has any questions about the last exercise.

Josh asks, "What if I read a script and don't feel anything, don't relate to the character at all?"

It's not easy to relate to every role you play, but that's the job. Some characters take more work than others. I think for a moment before asking: So what have you done in the past when you've had a character you didn't relate to?

"I panic a bit. But then I get the lines down so I'm word perfect, saying them over and over to myself so I'm okay to audition. I eventually start to feel more like the character doing that … and I research."

So you found that your own way. You have good instincts and I saw that in the cold read you did with Asia in the class on emotion. You might like to try this first-impression exercise, which is about using instinct. It gives you that extra bit of time to find a moment you relate to. It can help you feel: "Yes, I can do this. I have something there." And less panic!

Actors can sometimes be too hard on themselves and expect to get the acting right instantly. Be patient. Ask questions, trust your instincts, and put in the work.

Now, let's move on to the next exercise, a character improvisation.

## DEION

Kevin (Deion) walks quietly onto the stage from the side stage door, holding a basketball, into a living room environment he has set up.

He's exhausted. He calls out, "You home, Mama?" He waits: no answer. He walks quietly to the side of the stage and looks off as if seeing into another room, then eases back. "Nope" he says to himself. He whips off his backpack that's slung over his shoulder and lies spread eagle on his back.

After a moment, he throws the ball as if aiming toward a basketball hoop. He lets it bounce once then catches it. He does this for a while, then struggles back up.

Then with a sudden burst of energy he goes to an old cassette machine on the floor, puts in a cassette, and presses play. The recording sounds like old vinyl: Louis Armstrong playing "Mack the Knife" on trumpet. He listens to the song for a few beats, then conducts an imaginary orchestra completely involved and loving it.

When the music finishes Kevin grabs a man's jacket off a chair and puts it on. He stands tall, checking himself in an imaginary mirror at the front of the stage—the fourth wall of the room. Satisfied with how he looks …

He starts singing using the same gravelly voice as Louis Armstrong. After a moment, he gets into the song and cuts loose like a natural showman, caught up in the rhythm and hitting the notes perfectly. He finishes up with a big "Oh Yeah."

When I see that he is done, I say: Let's hear what you set up, Deion.

He moves his chair closer to the rest of us.

"I wanted to see what it felt like to be Kevin in his normal life before all that happened to him. So I set up a situation when he was at home alone. I had to use my imagination, because none of the interviews asked him about his life at home. According to neighbors, he was a good kid, so I figure he wasn't spending his time on the streets, getting into trouble. He'd be busy working toward his goals of playing trumpet and pro basketball. I can't play the trumpet, but I wanted to get the feel of being a musician like Kevin is. My great uncle's a jazz musician. When I asked who the greatest trumpet player was, he said Louis Armstrong. I listened to him on YouTube. He also sang, which gave me an idea of what to do.

"Imitating playing an instrument didn't feel right. So I thought if I imitated Louis singing I'd feel immersed in that kind of music, like it must feel when playing the trumpet. Oh, and I used how my character moves from the first exercise."

Well done, Deion, I tell him. You have a great voice. This is a big plus for the range of characters you can play.

I ask if he discovered anything about his character during the improv.

"What was interesting about singing was that I became a different person. Not just my voice and body, but my personality changed. It was like adding another dimension to where I felt quiet and shy. It's always interesting when I see someone at school standing back. You know, not drawing attention to themselves.

"Then suddenly I see them performing onstage in a band or something, and this whole new, charismatic personality appears. Even though Kevin seems quiet, he has strength. The singing helped me feel strong like I was somebody going places. It was a way of acting out my dream of being a famous musician. I don't know if Kevin would do that, but it helped me find another side to him."

I take a moment to ponder what I saw before offering my feedback.

Overall, I say, I saw a boy looking forward to a bright future; he has ambitions and works at it. And you made discoveries. You found a way to relate to Kevin's musical abilities, found his strength and dream in life. And you put your research to work. Well done!

Now, for the next character improv I'd like you to set up a situation with some close relationships in your character's life.

I'm sure some classmates can help you. And explore any questions you have about him from when you did your research.

"Okay, I'll do my best."

I look around, and it's clear the others want in on this. "Who has questions?"

Hayley asks, "So we imagine the character's life before they appear in the script and act that?"

Yes. When setting up your improv, ask how your character became who they are. Use clues from the script, but not the situations in it. Look at relationships, but not with characters you meet for the first time during the story. You can improvise with characters from the script if they've been part of your character's life before. Your job is to build your character's background. Like writing a biography, but with acting instead of words.

Asia asks, "We do these improvs before working on actual scenes in the script?"

Yes, I answer. The reason for the improvs is to prepare your character to be able to think, feel, and act in any circumstance. That way, even if the scenes in the script change, you'll know how to adjust. So you're ready with your role before the movie begins.

Many actors do preparation exercises beforehand, like living in the character's environment or with the people who've gone through what the character has—or the actor works the same job as the character.

You can act like the character as you go about your daily life, trying to do everything the way that character would: eating, dressing, talking to friends. It's about feeling truthful as another person and feeling like their life is part of you. Your present behavior is influenced by things that happened to you in the past. It's the same with your characters. These improvs help you create the character's history and condition you to behave like they would in any given situation.

Maya asks, "Can I work out what to act for scenes in the script just from analyzing it?"

I answer: You can get to a certain point with analysis. I can give you a list of analysis questions to help. And talking to the writer is always helpful, to better understand their intentions with the character. But my suggestion is to put whatever ideas you have into action and see if they work. That includes ideas that come from analysis. In all cases, it's best if you rehearse alone before doing it with other actors.

The essential thing about doing these exercises is discovering what you don't know about a character. If the writer included everything about the character's life in the script, it would be a book. Actors need to think beyond the writing and fill in the blanks. The writer put a lot of work into creating the story. It's your job to bring those words to life.

You do that by drawing on what you discovered when acting the character's background. Just as Deion did when he immersed himself in singing, working on his character's goals. He experienced what his character loves and dreams of becoming. So when he plays the character in the story, it will be devastating to see how the wrongful conviction destroyed everything he hoped for.

Jacob says, "So it's good to imitate a person, like Deion did with the singing?"

You can imitate to help create different behaviors in yourself, I say. But you need to practice it until you feel like it is part of you.

When you create a character, you work on the things about them that are different from you. In Deion's case, he imitated to feel like a musician. All that helped Deion change for the role. And he found strength in his character.

In acting, you can try any idea if it helps you relate to the character and become the role. Acting is the art of transformation. These improvs are one way to do that.

Before we move on to our next class [I turn to the class], if you haven't already, please exchange phone numbers so you can help each other with the improvs and scene work.

# CHAPTER 6

## CHARACTER BACKSTORY IMPROVISATION

Actors:

| | |
|---|---|
| Asia—improv as Angie, Kevin's sister | Deion—improv as Kevin |
| Maya—improv as a sister | Jacob |
| Hayley | Josh |

Onstage, a few chairs are arranged around a table with schoolbooks, pens, and a writing pad on top. The basketball rests in a corner of a living room setup.

Deion stands still onstage, preparing himself. His emotions surface. He holds them back. Then he begins the improv.

KEVIN (Deion) grabs the basketball and dribbles in place. He concentrates as he pounds the ball at knee height, then lower.

ANGIE (Asia) and MAYA (sister) come in from the side stage door. Angie says, "Hey, birthday boy, aren't you meant to be doing homework?"

"Sorry," he says, embarrassed, and grabs the ball.

Maya gives Kevin a quick kiss on the cheek. "Happy birthday. I have stuff to do, will see you in a bit." She goes back out the door.

Angie pulls a brochure from her handbag and drops it on the table. She gives Kevin a quick hug. "But before we celebrate …" She picks up the writing pad.

"Have you done any of your homework? I don't see anything," she says.

Kevin shrugs, head down. Fiddling with the ball.

Angie softens. "Come here," she says, and pulls out two chairs. She pats the seat beside hers. They sit. "Aren't you supposed to do an essay on your goals?" Angie asks gently.

Kevin shrugs and picks up the brochure. He glances at it, puts it down again.

"Why haven't you written anything?" Angie asks.

Kevin speaks quietly. "I don't know."

Angie reaches out and turns his face to look at her. "Has something happened?"

Kevin is afraid but covers. "I don't think I should write it. It's not important."

"Not important? Of course it is." She picks up a pen from the table and holds it in front of him.

Kevin looks at the pen but doesn't take it. "But … what if we have to read it to the class? Our teacher makes us do that. And we never know who'll have to read. We just sit there hoping it'll be somebody else."

Angie looks at him like they've have had this conversation before.

Kevin knows she expects him to say more. "I can't ... I can't read in front of everyone. It's embarrassing. And if I do say what I want to do, I'm not sure I can or even if it's possible, even though I want to, you know, get there. Everything takes money. What if my goals are something I can never have? So when I say what they are then I don't reach them, everyone will think I'm no good. I should just not say anything."

"Oh, boy," Angie says. "You sure know how to spin a story that hasn't happened ... but is that what you want, deep in your heart?"

Kevin doesn't answer.

Angie picks up the brochure. "Let's look at this so you can read about Syracuse University. We can apply—"

"Syracuse? How?"

Angie is gentle but firm. "You just have to work hard. And we have to work twice as hard as anyone else. You know that. Don't forget you have as much right to go there as anyone else. And I don't want to see you looking for a paycheck doing bad things on the street. You're good. I want to see you stay that way. Look at Charles Rangel. He was born in Harlem, went to college and law school, and now he's a congressman."

Kevin panics. "I don't want to be a congressman!"

"President, then?" Angie teases.

Kevin shakes his head. "As if."

"Then what do you want to do?" she asks.

Kevin seems embarrassed. Angie takes his hands. "Come on. I'm here for you; you know that."

Kevin hesitates, then speaks softly. "A trumpet player. And I want to play basketball ball for college." He looks at the brochure. "But you knew all along."

"I did." Angie says. "I just wanted you to say it out loud and not be afraid. So moving on, I asked around and what I learned was it's best to get a scholarship that's part athletic and part academic. So you need to get good grades. That way if you get hurt playing basketball, you have some backup."

Kevin remains nervous, uncertain.

"Nothing will happen to you, but you need to know the facts," Angie says. "You'll get paid if you're good enough. And you will be. You just need to believe that your dreams are possible, and work for them."

Kevin fiddles with the brochure, thinking.

"If you don't want to write this essay for yourself, will you do it for us, your family?" Asia says. "Please?" She hands him the pen.

Kevin takes it reluctantly. "What about being a trumpet player?" He's on the edge of his chair now, looking young and vulnerable.

Angie melts. "That makes me scared for you. There are a lot of bad people and bad drugs in the music world. But maybe they have a marching band at Syracuse. I can find out. Let's start with the essay, though, all right?"

Kevin surrenders. "Okay, but I hope I don't have to read it to the class."

"Just be proud of your goals. How about you practice reading it to me first, so you get used to being in front of people—just in case you are asked?"

Kevin nods.

Angie gives him a sisterly hug. "Back in a minute." She heads to the side door of the stage where she came in.

Kevin looks after her, wondering what she's doing. After a while, he pulls the writing pad close and is about to start writing when Angie comes back in with a cake sporting fourteen candles, singing "Happy Birthday." She is followed by Maya singing too and carrying a box.

Angie puts the cake on the table. "Make a wish."

Kevin closes his eyes, tears glistening on his cheeks. Finally, he opens his eyes and blows out the candles. He stands up and pulls the girls into a hug. "I never want to leave you."

Maya says, "We'll always be together."

Kevin laughs, overcome with emotion. He releases the girls.

Maya opens the box she brought with her and takes out a CD player and CD. "No more cassettes for you. Happy birthday." She plugs in the CD player and presses play; eighties dance music starts up.

Angie starts dancing. Maya pulls Kevin onto the floor with them. They dance.

After the improv winds down, I ask the actors to take a seat and tell us about what they set up and discovered. Deion goes first.

## DEION

Deion begins with, "I had some questions I wanted to explore. My first question was: How did the police know to pick on Kevin and the other four boys? Why them? They brought in other kids for questioning and let them go. I wondered what it was about my character that he'd make a false confession.

"In my research, I heard Kevin's lawyer say detectives are trained to get people to confess by whatever means possible:

violence, threats, anything. They lied to Kevin, telling him one of the other boys saw him attack the woman in the park. He didn't know he had the right to stay silent or ask for a lawyer. He didn't even know what a sex crime was until the detectives explained it to him in the interrogation."

So, I say, are you questioning if something in his character led him to be a police victim? Or made it easier for them to victimize him?

"Made it easier to victimize him," Deion says. "They tricked him, made him helpless. I don't see him as someone who thinks of himself a victim. You tell us to look at the character's future, how they work toward that and how they end up. Kevin Richardson is a survivor. He has a family now and helps other innocent prisoners get released through the Innocence Project. That's the opposite of being a victim.

"Another question I had was about how the detectives promised Kevin he could go home if he said what they wanted him to say. Why was going home so powerful for him? I wanted to explore his life at home to find out. I imagined his fourteenth birthday, because birthdays are a time when family show their love. I called Asia and Maya and asked them to play my sisters. The only one I knew anything about was Angie from the series. I told Asia she was the oldest sister, Angie, and a bit motherly. It was my birthday, a school day, and she knew I had to do an essay on goals.

"Maya and Asia had both seen the series, so I didn't have to explain everything. And I'm playing the same character they saw in my first improvs. I didn't tell them what to do or say; I just said 'improvise.' They gave me so much to work with, it was incredible." He turns to Asia and Maya. "You were great. Thank you."

Deion addresses the whole class again. "They completely surprised me with the brochure and that cake, and with the CD. The love they gave me got to my heart; it didn't feel like acting. It made me cry because they were so understanding and loving.

"I kept working on Kevin's youth and quietness, being a good kid, so I set up doing homework. And Kevin said he was shy. I read that shyness is the fear of what people think, of new things and situations. Of being in front of people and not fitting in. So just before the improv, I prepared for fear."

How did you prepare, I ask?

Deion says. "I tried various images first. Then I remembered being at my cousin's house, sitting by the pool. My auntie asked me to watch my cousin for a moment while she went into the house. He was only three and happy riding his tricycle around the pool. I'd been reading some audition sides. I put the pages down to watch him when the wind blew them away.

"I ran to pick them up, and when I turned around he was in the pool trying to keep his head above water. I dragged him out … for a long time after that I imagined what could have happened if I hadn't turned around and seen him, which terrified me. Seeing his little face just above the water freaks me out to think about it. That's the image I used for my preparation to get into feeling fear. I don't know how I could ever face anyone again if something had happened."

Your cousin is fine, right? I ask.

"Thankfully."

It is an intense preparation, I say, but you know not to dwell on it, yes?

"Right," he says.

How did your preparation affect you in the improv? I ask.

"The fear affected everything," he says. "How I related to my schoolwork, my future, my sisters ... how I thought and felt, even the way I see the world. What surprised me was when I held back from answering Angie because I was afraid. Then when I did speak, more came out than I expected. I felt I could go on and on with the story about not writing the essay.

"That helped answer a question I had about how Kevin could make up the story he did at the police station so they'd let him go home, when he was so shy. First, the police fed him a lot of details. Then he kept saying what he thought they wanted to hear. And he made things up, too. Something he said stuck in my mind. I can't think of the exact words, but he added to his confession. Fear would make somebody do that. I felt that happen in the improv. I wanted to make a strong impression on Angie with what I was saying, because I was afraid she wouldn't believe me if I didn't. So I just kept going. The detectives saw that Kevin was afraid. They used his fear to break him."

I nod. You've made huge steps relating to your character, I say. The image you used for the fear affected your thinking, feeling, and interaction in relationships. Use those feelings in all his scenes. Look for the opposite of fear, too, when he struggles to overcome it.

Acting on the questions you have about your character, you discovered more about him. You're finding your way with him. Working on how he acts in his life, you motivated a different side of yourself. We still see Deion, but in another way. There was a beautiful moment when you said, "I never want to leave you." That seemed spontaneous, but I think it answered a lot of questions about Kevin. Can you tell us what happened in that moment?

"Absolutely," Deion says. "It surprised me when I said it, but I think it's the key to why I would make a false confession. The detectives promised Kevin he could go home, and he was willing to do anything to get there. In the series, I saw a loving family. So I set up a family situation to find out what it felt like to act with them. Birthdays are special, so I tried that. Angie and Maya made me feel so loved. I panicked at the thought of losing them.

"I didn't ask them to love me like that, but they did. Angie was strong and kind at the same time. I felt like I had someone to encourage and support my dreams. The way she opened me up made me feel close to her. I'd definitely need her in a crisis."

When you said, "I'd definitely need her," do you think that was a temporary need in the situation, to be with those he loves? Or do you consider love to be his primary need in life? A character's need is what drives a person to achieve their goals. Given a choice, would it be love, ambition, or revenge that motivates him?

Deion takes a moment to think it over. "Could you explain that for me?"

Let's look at ambition, I say. An ambitious person seems to think ahead and plot things out. They want to be the best at any cost, and the people around them can suffer because of that. If he was ambitious, he might have been able to think clearly. For example, if he confessed, the criminal record would destroy a lot of opportunities he might otherwise have, for the rest of his life.

"He wasn't able to do that," Deion adds.

I continue: If he was a vengeful character he'd be doing destructive things to himself or others. That's not what I have seen in your interpretation of him so far. Maybe after he was sentenced to five to ten years in prison. That could have made him angry, wanting to get back at people and take revenge.

Deion says, "Not that either. From what I researched, after Kevin was released he kept on a good path. I think he wanted to do the right thing to make up for the pain he and his family felt from all of it. And now he helps people who've been through the same kind of thing. So I'm going to play the character so that love drives him—as a kid it was his music and basketball, his family, and as an adult his children and to help others. At least, that's the way I see it."

I'm impressed at the depth of that, coming from a sixteen-year-old.

You have terrific insight, Deion. If you were acting the role, you'd have behavior around loving your family and the fear of losing their love. For example, how would it make you feel if the prosecutor played the confession tape in court, and you had to watch your family sitting there listening to it?

"Devastated," Deion says. "But doing the improv taught me more about how much his family means to him. I love my own family, but to get to feel love in an imaginary situation in the improv was a terrific feeling."

Jacob raises his hand. "Is it possible to have two needs? What if I have a strong desire to be an actor because I love it, but I also have the ambition to be a success at it? Isn't that love *and* ambition?"

It's a question that comes up a lot in my coaching. I ask: If your parents said you weren't allowed to act anymore, how would you behave?

Jacob answers, "If my parents said I couldn't do acting, I'd try to reason with them and keep asking. But if they still said no, I don't think I'd want to hurt them or make problems until I got my way. I'd do what they asked. Because I love them. So I guess love is stronger than my ambition."

Deciding the primary need that drives a character helps you make clear choices when you portray them, I say.

I look to Deion. Is there anything you want to add?

"I did have another question about my character, but I think I found the answer when I worked on his shyness. Kevin said that being allowed to tell his story in interviews and the Ken and Sarah Burns documentary helped him "find his voice." To me that is meaningful because it means a person's true self, the voice inside that can be expressed for others to hear, and I feel sure and believe in what I have to say.

"So I thought: When didn't my character have a voice? Did he have a voice before the arrest, when he was young? I discovered in the improv that it was a struggle to admit my dreams. Like when I said, what about being a trumpet player? And Asia said no way. I let her divert my attention to the essay and wasn't confident enough to insist on what I wanted."

I also noticed a change in your voice, I add. You speak with confidence, but as the character, as well as being quiet you had a more even tone.

"Yes, I worked on that after I saw Kevin's interviews," Deion says.

Great, Deion, I say. At sixteen, you're asking questions and exploring characters. Making discoveries and learning about yourself and what side of yourself to use. Also gaining insight into human nature. Your hard work is paying off.

I look Asia and Maya. Let's hear how you prepared for the improv, I say.

## ASIA and MAYA

They look at each other. "You go first," Asia says.

Maya nods. "Asia and I got together and did some research. I borrowed a CD player and some old CDs for the music from my grandma. It helped a lot when we looked at an old documentary on Harlem in 1989. There was a teen girl who said, 'If you have a family of love, there's no need for the streets.'

"So seeing Deion working on his goals in the improvs and being a good kid at home made us feel certain that we are a loving family. So we tried to do that."

Asia adds, "And a street boy said if you 'do the right thing, respect people and work hard, you'll go far.' We wondered if any famous people from Harlem could be role models for doing well. We read about Congressman Rangel. Even though it was Kevin's birthday, we decided that the note to 'work hard' and his essay on goals were important too.

"The way Deion played Kevin really got to me when he said sorry about bouncing the ball. He looked so young and vulnerable. And I believed his fear. There was no way I could be mad at him when I saw the empty page. It made me want to help him. When Deion told me about the improv and said my character was motherly, I thought about my mom and the way she talked to my little brother. He had a hard time at school, but she encouraged him to keep going and sat there with him doing his homework and asked questions to help him come up with the answers. So I kind of did that with Kevin. But I learned a lot too."

That's good, I say. You and Maya have both done some excellent work here; the extensive research and how you saw the sisters' characters really helped make this improv come alive.

And you did what you need to in all improvs, which is set up the circumstances to act in: who you are, where you are, what you're doing, when, why, and how you behave …

Asia, I believed you as the older sister. Your observation of your mother's behavior gave you what you needed to do that. And by playing the opposite of what Kevin was feeling, you created conflict. Conflict doesn't always mean crisis. It can be what you did: having opposite feelings. Kevin was fearful and wanted to hide his thoughts, and you were confident and encouraging, helping him to open up. That made him decide whether to stick to what he thought or listen to you and overcome his fear. Which he did—and then he set out to do the essay. Both of you, great job.

I turn to the class and say: We saw how Deion set up his character with his fears and dreams. The dream is like a goal in life, which may not be achieved by the end of the script. It's what the character desires for their future. An actor needs to imagine the character's past and think beyond what happens in the story. Think of a movie script as a slice of the character's life. I'd like you to explore this idea when working on a role.

For example, a person's fear of not being good enough to reach their goals creates a struggle to overcome fear and work toward attaining their dream. The character has an inner battle with themselves as well as outer conflict in situations. Kevin's inner struggle affected everything he did. His character is a shy person, but even if he wasn't, there's an underlying side of human nature that fears we'll never have what we want.

We saw Kevin struggle to talk about his goals with Angie and write about them in an essay. But when he was alone and sang like he was onstage, he wasn't afraid. Because there he's expressing his dreams in private. So we saw two different ways he behaved, around the fear and the dream. Those are different aspects of his personality.

You could take away the words in Deion's improvs and still understand his character by what he did. As an actor, you can't just depend on dialogue. You create a visual story with your behavior.

In your scripts, look at how your character's fear and dreams affect your thoughts, feelings, *and* actions, through your expression in the dialogue and interactions with other characters. Even in silent moments. Onscreen you have many opportunities to play silent moments in your reactions and your close-ups. And the private moments where you reveal inner thoughts the other characters may be unaware of.

When working on a role, it helps to take some time to sit quietly and run the character's life through your mind, imagining all the little details that could happen. Using your imagination is one of the best things about acting.

Hayley adds, "There is so much to learn and do."

It might seem like a lot, I tell her, but the more you act and work on different roles, the easier it gets. Take it slowly. Build your characters one step at a time. You don't have to include every exercise in every role you play. Just use what brings out the best in you.

# CHAPTER 7

## WORKING ON A MOVIE SCENE

Actors:

Asia—playing Angie          Deion—playing Kevin

Hayley                      Jacob—a journalist

Maya                        Josh

In this class, I say to the actors: Deion will do a movie scene incorporating all that he learned from doing his improvisations based on his research and imagination, to develop the true life character, Kevin Richardson, one of the "Exonerated Five."

I look at Deion. Ready?

"Yes," he says, "I set up the scene onstage before class. Asia and Jacob are in the scene too, but I just need a moment to prepare." Okay, I tell him. He heads out the side stage door. Jacob and Asia follow.

After a few moments, Deion walks back onstage and slides under a blanket on a couch made up as a makeshift bed. The scene begins.

INT. 1989—HARLEM—RICHARDSON HOUSE—DAY

KEVIN (Deion) is curled up on his bed under a blanket; his face is hidden under a pillow. Boys' clothes are draped over a chair; sports and music posters hang on the wall; a basketball sticks out from under the bed.

ANGIE. (Asia) (Calls out offstage) Kevin, are you up?

Kevin moves under the blanket. The door opens, and Angie walks in. She kneels beside the bed and tries to lift the pillow. He pulls it tighter.

ANGIE. There's someone here to see you.

KEVIN. I don't want to see anyone.

Angie is gentle.

ANGIE. The boy says he wants to help.

Kevin throws off the pillow and sits up, panicked, genuinely panicked.

KEVIN. No, Angie, I can't. The school was enough, with everyone knowing about me. I can't. I won't.

At that moment, the door opens wider.

JACOB (14) appears. He is intelligent, confident, and dreams of being a journalist.

JACOB. Um ... sorry, your other sister told me to come in.

Kevin controls his panic, checking out Jacob.

ANGIE. I'll leave you two to talk.

She heads to the door.

KEVIN. Wait! Angie!

Angie hesitates. We see her pain looking back at Kevin but she leaves.

Friendly and relaxed, Jacob holds out his hand to shake Kevin's.

JACOB. I'm Jacob.

Tentative, Kevin shakes Jacob's hand.

JACOB. Do you mind if I sit down?

He moves the clothes on the chair to the side and sits down without waiting for an answer. Kevin is suspicious.

KEVIN. I guess.

JACOB. I'm hoping we can talk. I've been reading about what's going on around here. I want to write a protest piece against what's being said about you guys in the press.

KEVIN. Why would you want to do that?

JACOB. People should know what the cops have done.

KEVIN. I don't want to talk to any writers.

JACOB. Okay, but I want you to know that other kids know what's up. People who don't have experience don't understand the police state we live in. I bet the cops used every weapon to coerce you into saying what they wanted to hear. And as for that creep demanding the death penalty—

Jacob stops himself, seeing that Kevin is visibly shaken.

Kevin's breathing changes; the emotion rises in his throat. He struggles to hold on.

JACOB. Sorry, sorry. I can have a big mouth. It gets me in trouble sometimes. But look, I don't know if it helps, but I can tell by looking at you that you couldn't hurt anyone.

Kevin bursts out:

KEVIN. That's not true! Look what I've done! To my family, me, the other kids.

He ducks his head, fighting back his tears.

KEVIN. I need to be alone now.

Jacob nods. He hesitates about getting up, then adds:

JACOB. But can I say one thing?

Kevin doesn't answer.

JACOB. It's the cops hurting all of you, not you. Your family loves you. I see it in their eyes. And the way they quizzed me on why I was here, they don't want another person to hurt you. They practically pushed me into the room when they knew I was on your side. Do you know what I want to do?

Kevin looks up and wipes his nose, trying to get his feelings under control.

Jacob jumps up from his chair, he's passionate.

JACOB. I want to walk over to the *Daily News* on East Forty-Second; burst into their little cubicles; rip up their persecuting, lying, racist, hate-filled articles; and smash their dirty old typewriters over their brainwashed heads. And print an article that tells the truth.

Kevin's feelings overtake him: he begins laughing and crying at the same time.

JACOB. True.

KEVIN. Good luck with that.

He wipes his face and checks out Jacob, who is utterly sure of himself.

KEVIN. You would do that?

JACOB. Sure I would.

KEVIN. I don't think that would help you get anything published.

JACOB. Maybe, with that rag anyway. But I will find a way.

KEVIN. (Beat). I don't know. I'd have to talk to the others, and we got lawyers …

JACOB. I understand, but if you change your mind …

He takes a notebook and pen from his pocket and writes.

KEVIN. Hey! What are you writing?

JACOB. My phone number, if you want to talk.

He tears off a page, hands it to Kevin.

KEVIN. Jacob. What you said helps.

Jacob gives Kevin a reassuring look and walks out.

Kevin watches him leave, then sits there thinking. He gets up, his foot on his basketball. He rolls it for a moment. Then he picks it up, and angry, he throws it hard against the wall. He snatches his sweatshirt and tugs it on.

Finally, he stands tall and steels himself to face going out.

When the scene ends, I ask the actors to take a seat and tell us what they set up, and what they discovered in the scene.

Deion, Jacob, and Asia take seats facing the class. I look to Deion. Let's start with you.

## DEION

"I wanted to use everything I've done so far: the behavior, Kevin's relationship with his family and need for love, and facing the end of his dreams for his life. I needed to explore what happened after the boys were arrested, but before they went to prison.

"First, I thought of doing a scene from the Ava DuVernay miniseries. Then Jacob asked if he could write a scene, and I thought that was a great idea. So we got together on it …

"One of the boys who went to prison with Kevin said, 'Other kids knew what was up.' That set us thinking. Kevin was out on bail for a year, and we wanted to explore what that might have been like for him. Facing people every day, reading the press, and just waiting for the trial. What he must have felt about his family going through all that … Then Jacob sent me the scene."

I'm impressed they thought to do all that. I look to Jacob.

"Deion inspired me," he says. "I couldn't have written that without seeing him develop Kevin's character. It needs more work. We didn't have much time and I had to research."

Deion chimes in. "The script was fantastic and it helped me find something I didn't expect."

"What was that?" I ask.

"When I worked on the scene alone, I could see how the writing took my character through a change. I knew how I'd feel initially because of my prep for fear. Then at the end, the character is angry. I could do that. But the moment where he changes from despair to facing life, I just couldn't get when working alone.

"Doing the scene with Jacob, I *felt* the change happen. What I didn't expect was crying and laughing at the same time. It brought me out of myself and helped me engage with Jacob. I felt my courage come back. I didn't feel like I was acting or planning it. Jacob played it like he was on a mission but charming and funny. I don't think he meant to be funny, but his passion for destroying the news office was. It was impossible to feel down around him for long.

"I felt myself change in those moments from wanting to shut out the world to deciding to listen to what he had to say. He helped me have enough strength to get through another day. It was like I was really in it."

I nod. Now you see the value of working on the character before acting the script, I say. Intellectually your character transitions from feeling despair to having enough courage to face the world. But in the scene, you felt the emotion organically and experienced the change like it was part of you. With all the preparation you've done, using different sides of yourself and in different situations, you've conditioned yourself to *be* your character in any circumstance. So you can interact with whatever another actor gives you.

Do you think you could repeat the moment of change you just discovered for another take? And let's say the other actor is not on set with you.

Deion concentrates. Then with tears in his eyes he begins to laugh.

I smile. Yes, you can repeat. Did you rehearse with Jacob?

"We didn't rehearse." Deion answers. "We played it like a movie shoot where the actors show up, meet for the first time, then do the scene. We read it through together a couple of times before class. I don't think I could have done the scene without the preparation exercises I did here. Like finding a way to feel the character's shyness. Or the image I could use for my feelings and realizing how much his family means to him, and Kevin's need for love. It's like all that was waiting inside me, somewhere, and it came up without me having to think about it in the scene …

"When working on the scene, there was something I did think about, though. And that was how to convey how tough it must have been for Kevin during that time. I only live with the feeling for a short time. Kevin lived it twenty-four seven for years. That must have had a huge impact, not just then but for the rest of his life. Is it even possible to convey that?"

His question calls to mind occasions when I'm coaching actors one-on-one in the opening moment of a scene, and I'm looking to feel the impact of the character's emotion right from the start. I turn to the class. Let's look at how actors can create impact, I say. In drama, a character goes through momentous problems in life and struggles to overcome them. Movie scenes are generally short, with a lot of information presented in a short period of time. The emotional impact from the actor needs to be strong; it needs to tell the story of the character's struggle with more than words alone.

To do this, you need a strong emotional preparation that will carry you into the scene. Then, right from the beginning of a scene, hold that emotion inside you. You will feel it but don't let it out yet. Doing the scene will add to your feelings and those watching will feel the impact of something happening to you. When you reach the crisis point where the character lets out all their feelings, the audience will understand what's happening and also what you were feeling at the start.

I tell Deion he did that with his emotional prep for fear. You made an impact, I add. The way you pulled the pillow harder around your head told us you were in a bad way.

Right from the beginning you were caught up in the drama of the situation and the struggle you faced. I believed your fear in the way you hid, your desperation to keep people out, and the pain you felt when you blamed yourself for what happened and what your family had to go through too. All of that told me you loved your family very much. The struggle to hold onto your feelings left me wondering if you'd be able to carry on, but you did.

The moment when Jacob made you laugh made it clear you weren't ready to give up. How you threw the ball told me your strength had returned. You went from fear to courage, and we saw a survivor emerging. As well as all the behavior you worked on in your improvs: a boy of fourteen, filled with shyness and vulnerability, and a boy whose greatest need is love and greatest fear is losing love. Did you use the same emotional preparation you did with your improvs?

Deion nods. "I needed to find a way to relate to the fear Kevin must be in about what could happen to him. I used the image of seeing my little cousin fall in the pool and almost drown because I looked away. But I took the image even further and imagined he drowned. It freaked me out. I wanted to disappear. I made a choice that my character wanted to disappear, and that's why I hid under the blanket."

I take that in. Adding the imaginary thought was courageous, I say. The imaginary image combined with a real situation from your past summoned powerful feelings. Acting demands that you feel as deeply as the character should, and you clearly did that. Even though you had tears, you chose to hold back your feelings and not completely break down. That worked for your character in his present state because the worst is yet to come for him.

Always have more feelings than you need, I say. Then you have more control over how much you let out. Your instinct worked because your character is still at a time in his life where he hopes he won't be convicted.

"Right," Deion says. "For this scene, we decided the 'trial by press' is affecting him more than anything else. But there's still hope. Even though he told the police he was at the scene, he told them he didn't do the crime. And there was no DNA evidence. Then later on when he was offered a deal to plead guilty, he turned it down. So he must have had some hope still."

When he's convicted, I add, that's where he'd completely break down because all hope is lost. When you analyze your scripts, look at how the character progresses through the story; find the crisis moment and build toward it. How do you see your character now? Has he grown since you did your first behavior and backstory improvs?

"Definitely." Deion says. "The seriousness of his situation has way more effect on me now. It's like everything I hope for gets destroyed, and it's my fault because of what I said to the detectives."

I tell Deion he's doing serious work. Your bravery in using a painful motivation and exploring the character's tragic situation shows your willingness to face challenges head-on. You've been working since your preteens. Now you're ready to transition to adult work and more complex roles that require deeper skills. I'd like to congratulate you. It is a joy to see you grow into such a fine actor.

Deion grins. "Thank you. It is quite a ride."

I nod and turn to Jacob. Okay, Jacob, let's hear from you now.

## JACOB

Jacob breathes out: "Phew! I got through it. Don't get me wrong; I had a great time, but I was nervous. I said to myself, just let it happen and go with whatever comes up. Even though I wrote the scene, I had to drill myself on the lines so I'd be free to act … so what did I prepare for the scene?

"After Deion agreed I could write the scene, I did some research and tried to incorporate what he's been working on. I looked at the newspaper headlines from 1989 and couldn't believe all the articles condemning Kevin and the other boys. It was like the press put them on trial. It made me angry. If I was living in that time, I wouldn't want to sit around feeling helpless. I'd want to do something to help. So I decided to use that feeling in a scene. I came up with the idea of being a young journalist who wants to write a story about one of the boys, as a sort of protest against all the bad stories that were kind of rushing to judgment. I wrote what I believe and wound up playing a version of myself."

Jacob, I say, this is intelligent and well-thought-out work, the writing and acting.

You used your own moral convictions and added them to an imaginary situation.

Acting the scene, I believed you as a young journalist, fervently believing he can get his side of the story told. Your behavior told the story of a confident boy on a mission. We could see that when you sat down before Kevin agreed, and in the way you stayed positive even though you didn't get the story. You created conflict by having opposite feelings from Deion's character. When he was down, you were encouraging. And you tried different ways to persuade Kevin to talk about his experience: you were friendly, apologetic, sympathetic, and angry toward others. That was right, too. When acting, you look at all the different ways the character can get his needs met. Your wanting to help was clear.

Jacob adds, "What I found difficult when working on a true story was that I needed to imagine things to feel it and make it work on page and stage."

I agree. It's impossible to know everything about someone when working on a true story, I say. But your research built a history for your character to act from, which you did sincerely and with conviction.

And I agree with Deion. You are charming, and that will always work for you in your acting. But I know, after seeing what you did with your character and the thought you put into the writing and performance, that you won't rely on charm alone. You'll work hard at everything. Fantastic scene, Jacob.

## ASIA

I turn to Asia and ask to hear from her. She's happy to talk.

"I loved doing the scene," she says. "I loved working with these guys. So for this scene, I wanted to be loving and tread carefully so I didn't hurt Kevin, but I knew I'd have to be firm to try and get him out of his depression. And like I did before in the improv, I played it like my mom."

I give her my perspective. In both the improvisation in the last class and the scene, I say, I believed your love for Kevin. Observing your mom then acting that behavior in an imaginary situation enhances your ability to play different characters. You were gentle but firm … There was a private moment at the door where I saw the concern you felt for Kevin. We the audience saw it, but Kevin didn't because Jacob distracted him. Did you plan that?

Asia says, "When Kevin called my name, I felt bad for leaving. So I looked back at him. I wanted to stay with him, but the script says I leave. So I justified that by thinking: no, can't stay, he has to deal with some things without me."

I nod. Revelatory moments like this work well on screen. It gives the audience insight into your character, what you're thinking and feeling that's not put into words. So, again, you did terrific work.

I look to the class. Does anyone have any comments?

Maya speaks up, addressing Deion. "I wonder about when you burst out about what you'd done and struggled to keep from breaking down. Did you plan to have all that emotion at that particular moment?"

"No plan." Deion says. "I felt the emotion when I did my prep before the scene. Then acting the scene added to my feelings. When I first started acting I was always thinking ahead, planning to do this and that in specific places. Now I just let it happen. When Jacob said that line about the death penalty, that shocked me; the words had a huge impact. I could barely speak. I felt my whole body change, and I teared up. I had to work hard to hold back. Then my feelings got mixed up with him making me laugh. But I don't think the scene would have affected me as much if I didn't have the emotional preparation beforehand. It helped me relate and feel like the character."

"Thanks, Deion," Maya says.

Josh asks, "My question is for Jacob. When you called Deion, did you have an idea about the scene you wanted to write?"

Jacob thinks that over. "Kevin's struggle at that point in his life and how he was holding up were what I thought about. Then one night at home, I was thinking about the story, and the image came to me of Kevin retreating into himself, completely depressed. So I went from there. And it helped to see Deion working on Kevin's character, his shyness and how that made him act."

I ask Jacob if he thought of the character first, and the scene grew out of that?

"Yes," he says. "Deion and I both worked from that point of view."

What you did is correct, I say. It's the character that drives the story ... There are other questions that an actor can ask when studying a scene, like: "What would my character be doing if the other characters weren't there?" And "What is this moment in the character's life?" For example, look at the scene the actors just did. You could take Jacob out of it and Kevin would still have his problems, and maybe he'd have to find a way to move forward on his own. The actors were right to create a scene with the lead character having both inner and outer struggles.

The actors nod and take notes. Josh asks Deion, "When you did your first impression exercise and you felt how your character moves, did you have to think about that when you did the scene?"

Deion considers this. "When I did the emotional prep, it put me in the mindset to make me shy, which affected how I moved and spoke. So I don't have to think about it when I'm in it. Which is strange because at first, it was my body telling me what felt right. But now it feels natural to behave that way. At least on the stage."

Hayley speaks up. "That scene was so great, thank you. What I take from this is that no matter how bad things are for the character and how emotional they are, we can act it without hurting ourselves. Like Deion is sitting here now, calmly discussing how he acted the character's painful situation. Sometimes in the past, I'd hold onto my feelings for hours so I'd be ready when it was time to shoot the scene. This one time I remember I wouldn't eat lunch or talk to anyone. The on-set teacher was mad at me, and my mom was worried about me. And when it came time to do the scene, I'd lost all the feeling. That wasn't a good day."

I agree. You need to be very careful not to overwork your emotion, I say. Motivate your feelings when your character needs them, just before a scene. The hardest thing to do is to have faith that your preparation will work for you. As Deion said, he just lets it happen now. If what you expected doesn't come up, use what feelings you already have. That will ensure your acting is sincere and from the heart. After the scene, let go of those feelings. Eat lunch or do something else that's totally different.

I turn to the class.

After these last three classes on character development and scene work, I hope you can see the purpose of developing a character before you act the script. You don't want to come to the end of the shoot and feel like you finally discovered your character, just then. You need to be ready on day one. It's natural to experience changes along the way, but you can adjust while in character.

Because movies are shot out of sequence, it helps to do emotional prep before each scene to motivate the character's frame of mind, so the progression of your character in the final edit makes sense. To help you do this, I suggest that after studying the script, you remove your scenes and lay the pages out on the floor so you can see your character's journey through the story. Imagine any events that are *not* in the script but that could affect your character before or after a scene.

Finally, when you memorize the dialogue, do it quietly at first so you don't get stuck saying things a certain way. Then once you've learned the lines, you're free to act and add in all your character's thoughts, feelings, and actions. The character's way of speaking will arise spontaneously, based on all of that. Then you're ready to shoot the movie.

# CHAPTER 8

### A SCENE ON CAMERA

Actors:

| | |
|---|---|
| Hayley— playing Ophelia | Josh—working the camera + reader |
| Maya | Deion |
| Asia | Jacob |

JOSH SETS UP A TRIPOD AND CAMERA ON THE STAGE IN FRONT of Hayley, who is dressed as Ophelia.

Hayley does emotional prep for her character: Ophelia. After a moment, she nods to Josh. He picks up a script and stands by the camera, ready to read the other characters in the scene, the queen and king. He hits RECORD.

### HAMLET, ACT IV, SCENE V

OPHELIA wears a long white dress, torn shreds hanging here and there. Her hair is messy, her eyes glazed over. She looks around, as if searching for someone.

OPHELIA. Where is the beauteous majesty of Denmark?

QUEEN. How now, Ophelia?

OPHELIA. (Sings) *How should I your true love know, From one another? By his cockle hat and staff, And his sandal shoon.*

QUEEN. Alas, sweet lady, what imports this song?

Ophelia steps forward, angry. She looks right into the queen's eyes.

OPHELIA. Say you?

After a moment, she gasps and gazes at something that's not there.

OPHELIA. Nay, pray you mark.

She drifts back.

OPHELIA. (Sings) *He is dead and gone lady, He is dead and gone, At his head a grass-green turf, At his heels a stone. Oh ho.*

QUEEN. Nay, but Ophelia—

OPHELIA. Pray you, mark.

Her hand reaches out to touch what she thought she saw. She tears up, sliding her hand over the length of the shroud she imagines before her.

OPHELIA. (Sings) *White his shroud as the mountain snow.*

QUEEN. Alas, look here, my lord.

OPHELIA. (Sings) *Larded all with sweet flowers, Which bewept to the ground did not go, With true-love showers.*

KING. How do you, pretty lady?

Ophelia is confused hearing another voice. Then, seeing the king, she focuses on him.

OPHELIA. Well, God reward you.

Her expression grows threatening.

OPHELIA. They say the owl was a baker's daughter. Lord, we know not what we are but know not what we may be. God be at your table.

KING. Brooding upon her father.

Ophelia covers her face with her hands.

OPHELIA. Pray, let's have no words on this—

She looks up with a jolt, hands grasping, as if holding something close to her heart.

OPHELIA. But when they ask you what it means say you this. (Sings). *Tomorrow is Saint Valentine's day, All in the morning betime, And I a maid at your window, To be your Valentine.*

She opens her hands, as if stung by what she heard.

OPHELIA. (Sings) *Then up he rose, and donn'd his clo'es, And dupped the chamber-door, Let in a maid, that out a maid, Never departed more.*

KING. Pretty Ophelia.

OPHELIA. Indeed without an oath I'll make an end on't.

She beats her chest with her fists while she sings.

OPHELIA. (Sings) *By Gis and by Saint Charity, Alack and fie for shame! Young men will do it if they come to't, By cock they are to blame. Quoth she before you tumbled me, You promised me to wed …*

She breaks off singing and looks into the distance, overcome with sadness.

KING. How long has she been thus?

OPHELIA. I hope all will be well. We must be patient, but I cannot choose but weep to think they would lay him i' th' cold ground.

She stands tall, proud.

OPHELIA. My brother shall know of it, and I thank you for your good counsel. Come my coach.

She signals her imaginary coach to come close, but her hand stops mid-gesture. She pauses, perhaps realizing where she is. Then slowly lowers her hand. With a wistful look at something invisible, she lightly steps back.

OPHELIA. Good night, ladies, good night. (Whispers). Sweet ladies, good night, good night. (Sings) *He is gone, he is gone, And we cast away moan, God 'a' mercy on his soul!*

Josh waits for a few moments before turning off the camera.

I ask Josh and Hayley to take a seat, and Hayley to tell us about her work on the scene. I let Josh know I'll want to hear from him too.

I look to Hayley. Good work, Hayley, I say. I'm excited to see you tackle Shakespeare, and I can tell you know *Hamlet* inside-out.

"I did what you said," Hayley tells me. "I read the play straight through. I didn't understand a lot of it. So my mom bought me *Shakespeare's Stories*. Reading a synopsis with some dialogue helped. Then I saw the *Hamlet* film you told us about, the black-and-white one. Laurence Olivier was easy to understand, which helped. The way he directed the film also helped me see that Hamlet and Ophelia really did love each other. There are shots where Ophelia sees him passing doorways in the castle, and I could feel her longing to be with him."

I ask: How do you see Ophelia now that you've worked on her?

"Suffering from loss is the main idea," Hayley says. "And delicate, which is what I felt happen after I did the spinning action in the first class, with the example you gave us of a girl exploring how to feel like Ophelia. Now that I know the play, that delicate feeling makes sense. Ophelia's mind breaks into pieces when she loses everyone she loves. A lot of my interpretation is based on that first exercise."

And what did you work on for the scene?

"Right from the beginning, when I did the spinning, it made me feel like I was off balance and couldn't think clearly. Like I was in a dream. You know how dreams feel broken up. Some of it's real and some not, and I grasp for what's happening. I thought that was a good approach for someone who's going mad. When I did my research, I understood what was happening in her mind. After that I could just bring up the physical feeling without having to spin around.

"My mom's a doctor, and she said Ophelia is one of those people who never gets past their grief after losing someone they love. They just keep focusing on the loss and can't move on. Sometimes they get depressed, and even die by suicide.

"I also wondered about what was causing the feeling I had of living in a dream. I learned that people hallucinate after suffering from shock. Ophelia must be feeling that because of what she experienced from Hamlet's rejection when he screams at her, saying women make men monsters and get to a nunnery, and then Hamlet murders her father. If that happened to me, I'd definitely be in extreme shock."

Did you make any discoveries while working on the scene itself? I ask.

Hayley takes a moment to think. "When Ophelia says, 'I'll make an end on it,' I wondered if that was her threatening suicide. But that didn't make sense because in the lines before and after, she talks about being a Valentine, and a man leaving a girl. So I decided to just rehearse the scene and imagine what was happening.

"When I called for the coach, I felt like I didn't know where I was for a moment.

When I backed away on the last goodnights, I felt like I wanted to drift away from this world forever. And she does in the end by letting herself drown."

I love what you created with your Ophelia, I tell her. Your movements were drifting and fragile. I remember what you said after the spinning exercise: that you felt delicate. I saw you struggle with your sanity, sometimes focused other times in a daze. It was a perfect choice to play her like you're in a dream. It helped you go in and out of reliving memories, seeing images, feeling pain, and anger at the queen and threatening the king. All mixed together, without logic.

That moment you discovered that she wanted to "drift away from this world forever." In that pause where your hand stopped. Then, as you slowly brought your hand down, it was like you'd decided something; that was a very clear transition with thought and action. Then seeing you step backwards, with the delicate movements and how you looked and felt … I believed that Ophelia wouldn't have the strength to face life anymore. You told us that story without words, which is great for movie acting.

Hayley nods. "I also think the weak feeling comes from Ophelia being submissive to her father's wishes. When I was studying the play, I never felt that she could speak up without being criticized. He forbids her to go near Hamlet, telling her he's a prince and won't marry her because she's not a royal. He crushes her so she can't think for herself. And he takes the precious letters Hamlet sent her and uses her to spy on him. He totally controls her."

I turn to the class. In that era, I say, women in Ophelia's social class depended on men to survive. Society expected women to be subservient, devoted mothers. And that's how Ophelia thought of herself. She treated the men in her life with respect and kept her feelings to herself until they drove her mad.

Hayley adds, "Once I understood the history, I could get the performance down. For me, acting, I have to believe what's happening in the story, and why the character is the way they are. Grieving, Ophelia probably doesn't eat much and loses her strength. She doesn't take care of herself either. That's why I decided her dress would be all torn, from climbing trees and reaching for flowers like the queen says she does."

I smile and tell her: Superb work on this character, Hayley. And remember, this is your interpretation of Ophelia, based on a physical action exercise and your imagination. You can learn from what other actresses have done with the role, but try not to compare yourself to them; have faith in the role you have created.

Now I'd like the class to make any comments or ask any questions they may have.

Maya jumps in. "Did you find Shakespeare's language hard?" she asks.

Hayley laughs. "I studied the words I didn't understand in the footnotes, which are on the bottom of the page in the play.

Once I knew what the words meant I could make better sense of the sentences. Then I memorized the scene. After that, I was free to act. I let the emotion I had and the actions I took affect the dialogue. Plus I made sure to speak clearly and put all my feelings into my voice, and that my feelings were deep. I learned that from the black-and-white movie.

Jacob asks, "What happened when you covered your face at the mention of your father?"

"I just followed an urge to do that," Hayley answers. "I don't know if you remember, but it happened in the first class too, after I did the physical actions. After Christine told us the story of *Hamlet*, it made me sad to think of Ophelia with no mother. But for the scene, I needed to feel the loss of her father, which is a deeper feeling than thinking about a mother she never knew or couldn't remember."

Jacob asks another question. "I saw you concentrating before the scene. Were you doing emotional prep to feel that loss?"

"Yes. I imagined losing a loved one who's been with me all my life. The emotion from that prep affected me whenever I talked about the father. Losing love is Ophelia's underlying feeling from the beginning of the play, when her father forbids her to see Hamlet, then her brother leaves for another country, and then after Hamlet murders her father the king banishes him from the country. And with no mother to turn to, she must have felt completely lost and alone, which added to her grief."

Asia asks, "If loss was your main emotional state, what helped you change feelings from anger, to tears, to threatening?"

Hayley thinks for a moment. "Shakespeare writes a lot of powerful images that I could run with, and those motivated my feelings. Like Ophelia's father in a shroud. But an image I saw on TV helped too. It was a police show where the daughter has to lift a white sheet to identify her mother's body. When she saw the face and realized her mom was gone forever, she broke down.

"I thought it must be like that for Ophelia. That image of the mother under the white sheet made Ophelia's situation more real for me because I've never experienced anything like that. And I worked on how I felt about my relationships with the queen, Hamlet, the king, and my brother."

Deion asks, "When your hands went to your heart in the Valentine song, it looked like you didn't want to let go of what you were holding. But then you let go as if something hurt you. Was that one of Hamlet's letters?"

Hayley nods. "Yes. In the Valentine song, the man breaks his promise to marry the girl. That must have reminded her of Hamlet. But even after he rejected her, she still loves him. She's more concerned about him acting insane around the royal court than she is with her own feelings.

"I imagined holding one of his letters close to my heart, to feel his love again. Then as I was singing '*Then up he rose*,' the song reminded me of his rejection, and that the letter was a lie. So I threw it away and acted how I really felt: hurt. It also helped my feelings to hold onto something, to squeeze my hands tight around it. It made me feel more."

Jacob asks, "What about the moment when you looked at the queen and seemed angry?"

Hayley says, "I was having some trouble with how I felt toward the queen. But then I had the idea: What if I imagined Ophelia was walking past the queen's bedroom and heard voices fighting, and she stopped to find out what was happening?

So I read the scene again where Hamlet and the queen fight and imagined myself standing in the doorway watching them. I imagined a sword going through the curtain and hearing a scream, then seeing my imaginary father fall through the curtain, covered in blood, and Hamlet holding a bloody sword.

"As I imagined what was happening and read the dialogue, I felt really angry because the only thing the queen says is 'What have you done?' The rest of the scene is about Hamlet telling his mother to stay away from her husband, the king. I realized they didn't care about Ophelia's father, or how Ophelia would feel when she found out. When I looked the queen in the eye, I was angry and blamed her for my father's murder. She shouldn't have let my father spy in her bedroom."

Maya asks, "What was the threatening look about when you spoke to the king?"

"Basically," Hayley answers, "she's saying to the king you never know what might happen to you. That thought comes from the dialogue when Ophelia says the baker's daughter was turned into an owl. The footnotes explained it was because she didn't give someone some bread. So she is punished, like the king might be. There's so much meaning in Shakespeare's writing that sometimes I can just let his words tell me what to do. He also writes that Ophelia beats her chest. When I did that, it felt like I was trying to stop my heart from aching."

Hayley, I say, you successfully developed a character by working toward how she ends her life. I saw her, and I saw you falling apart. You should be very proud of your Ophelia.

Hayley adds, "I meant to say too that I cut the dialogue for the scene to shorten it a bit and did her second-to-last scene in the play instead of the last. I felt like I could do more with her relationships in this scene."

I noticed, I say. And it worked well. It gave you way more to explore and think about.

I look to Josh. Now I'd like to hear how you and Hayley worked to record the scene.

Josh dives in. "When you told Hayley to do the Ophelia scene on camera, I asked her if I could help. Hayley sent me the scene to study so I'd be familiar with it when I read the other characters, and to help with recording it."

I turn to Hayley and ask: Can you tell us how you played off the other characters, when it was just Josh reading beside the camera?

"I looked at Josh" she says, "and tried to affect him with what I felt toward the queen and king. I didn't put a face on top of his, but I felt like I was talking to the characters all the same. And we made sure that he stood close to the camera so that when I was looking at him my face was in full view on the screen."

Did you look at how to add meaning to the story with the way you moved on camera?

"Yes, Josh helped me with that. We did the scene in one shot, like an audition on camera." Hayley looks at Josh.

Josh continues, "Before class, we worked on the moves. We started with a mid-shot when Ophelia looks around for the queen. When she took a step closer to the camera we did that so she'd be in a close-up when she looked angry facing the queen. We wanted to show that intensity to the audience, so they could see what Ophelia was thinking in her eyes.

Then she moved back into her mid shot. That way we could see actions like her reaching out to touch her father's shroud, her hands when she imagined holding Hamlet's letter close to her heart, and calling for the coach.

"When Ophelia stepped back into a long shot, we could see her full body movements. Then when she stood still at the end and kept her feelings going, I let the camera record a bit longer. In that moment we could see the full impact of Hayley as her character, Ophelia."

Good thinking, I tell him. Your explanation of how an actor can work within the frame and add meaning to the story is very helpful. Thank you both for all the work you put into this scene on camera.

I look at the class and tell them: You have now completed what we began in the first class, where we discovered what each actor needed to work on to maximize their talent. We did this by using a physical action, reaching out to touch an imaginary face in the air of someone you love to see how it affected you. Or with the other physical action of spinning around to see how it affected your mind and body. From that and throughout the following classes, you've explored how to find sides to yourself, motivate deep feelings, improvise and act scenes from the lives of complex dramatic characters.

Remember, the key to playing a dramatic role is to realize that the actor creates the drama. Dramatize whatever is at stake. Is it a life-and-death situation? And even if it isn't, does it feel that way to the character? If you're not reaching the depth of feeling needed for the scene, then make it a life-and-death situation, and that will affect everything you do. "Raise the stakes," as a director might say.

I pause, taking in the actors, young and eager, and ready to go out into their professional lives, acting.

I continue: We've now come the end of the course. You've all worked hard, fearlessly, imaginatively, creatively, and with great dedication to your acting. It's truly a gift seeing you in class as you explore your characters and make new discoveries about your own abilities and potential. Thank you.

# Acknowledgements

As with many things in my life this book would not been possible without the love, support, and guidance of others: My acting teacher, the late John Lehne, whose vast knowledge and insights into what it takes to be a great actor opened my eyes to our art, and for his guidance and faith in my ability to teach actors. A big thank you to all the young acting students who have ever studied with me and their parents, managers, and agents who believed in my teaching and coaching methods. To the actors who sent endorsements: Anna Jacoby-Heron, Kevin Sheridan, Michael Grant, and Jessye Romeo. To those who endorsed my work with actors: Fred Roos, an icon in the movie industry for casting and producing. Michele for her daughter, Kyla Kenedy. Chris Snyder, agent and manager, for his support and dedication to actors. Meredith Fine, Director of Youth Division Coast to Coast Talent Group, LA, and her team Dana Edrick Fletcher and Reagan Wallace. To Kevin Richardson, for graciously agreeing to a teen actor developing a role based on Kevin's true story and for it to be written about in this book.

Thank you, to my editor, John Robert Marlowe at The Editorial Department (TED), for his insights, and expertise, which guided me to make this book possible; and to Ross

Browne and Julie Miller, (TED). Caroline O'Connell for her expert marketing advice. My dear friend Maureen Connell Guillerman, a novelist, who helped me create a table of contents by synopsizing thousands of words in a chapter to create a heading. To Marianne, for the book cover design at Premade EBook Cover Shop, and to my granddaughters, Claire and Mia, for their artistic advice on the cover. Gabriella Regina at GR Book Covers for the format. To my daughter Anna and my son Anthony, for their incredible support in all I do. It has been quite a challenge to write a book on acting, but I persisted because I believe in and love the work I do with actors.

# Endorsements

"Working with Christine prepared me for the business in the best way possible. Her wealth of experience is incredible and I wouldn't be where I am in my career today without her. We worked on auditions in my early career and she helped me to analyse and breakdown scenes in a way that I use every time I prepare. Christine also helped me to hone my skills and gave me invaluable tools that help me get to where I need to when I'm on set and working under immense pressure. I learned things about working on camera with Christine before I booked jobs that required me to be on big sets and her words and techniques stay with me to this day. An incredible woman and a wonderful teacher. I am beyond grateful that our paths crossed."

—**Jessye Romeo,** *Robyn Hood series regular, Pennyworth, In the Long Run, Lucky Break.*

"Christine was my first teacher, the one that sent me on my path in life, and for that I am eternally grateful. From my days acting, to my days now putting pen to paper, the work we did together has informed who I am as an artist and an individual. How lucky I am to have had Christine in my life, and at such an early age. What I fondly remember most from our time working together was the time spent delving into the inner life and workings of a character. To this day, I still believe this is where the good stuff is. The gold. The stuff that makes a scene vibrate and change the air. And Christine showed me where to look."

—**Kevin Sheridan,** *Soulman with Dan Aykroyd, series regular. American Dreams series regular. Leaving Barstow, feature film, actor, producer, writer.*

---

"I BEGAN WORKING WITH CHRISTINE MCCLURE AS A TEENAGE actor in Los Angeles. At that time, I had worked extensively in TV and was starting to book work in films. Though I was working, I sensed I was at a point artistically and creatively where I needed to go deeper and develop a stronger craft that I could call upon to repeat performances and build characters.

When I first met with Christine, she was very supportive of these aims and we went to work immediately. Christine had such a wonderful and compassionate approach to teaching the craft of acting and engendered a great deal of trust and inspiration in our work together.

Specifically, I recall being very moved by the concept in character building of 'inner content' versus 'outer form'—the inner content encompassing the true desires, hopes, and needs of a character, and the outer form detailing the ways in which that would manifest itself in a character's exterior behavior. This was pivotal for me to grasp, as it began to enable me to build layered character work.

While it was significant to learn this intellectually, a trap for a young actor can be to keep the work in one's head without emotionally connecting to the character. To this extent, Christine taught me how to implement the techniques of affective memory. In short, affective memory is the process of stimulating memories from deep in the subconscious through the use of sensory elements to spark a present response to a past experience. The affective memory can be both real and imagined. Often times, I found the freedom to switch from the real to the imagined most effective for me personally. Through our work together, I discovered that I was at my best when freely mixing the real base from past experiences with imaginary elements from the character's circumstance to create a full affective memory. These affective memories would prove to be very powerful and could be done to build out key aspects of the character. Building a base of affective memories allowed me to make my performance very real and created a launching pad as a performer to be able to get on set, trust the work, and be fully in the moment with my fellow cast.

As I have transitioned primarily to writing/directing in recent years, I have continued to employ the framework and techniques I learned with Christine to construct fully three-dimensional characters. Inner content/outer form and building affective memories both have continued to be key parts of my process in building characters both in front and behind the camera."

—**Michael Grant,** *actor, writer, producer, composer. The Secret Life of An American Teenager, series regular. Fair Haven, feature film. HarisGrant Productions, producer, director.*

"Christine helped me understand the process of coming into my character and how to stay focused and ready on the set. She pushed me when she knew I could do more, anticipated what doubts and difficulties I would experience, and gave me ways to deal with them. Christine taught me so much about the movie-making details and the discipline it takes to be a professional actor. Our preparation work on my character gave me the confidence I needed. I came from our sessions together exhilarated, inspired, and in love with acting."

— **Anna Jacoby Heron,** *Contagion, with Matt Damon, feature film. Finding Carter, series regular. Dirty John, The First, series.*

www.ingramcontent.com/pod-product-compliance
Lightning Source LLC
Chambersburg PA
CBHW062114080426
42734CB00012B/2864